GoodFood

101 SPEEDY SUPPERS

10 9 8 7 6 5 4 3 2 1

Published in 2009 by BBC Books,
an imprint of Ebury Publishing
A Random House Group company

Recipes © BBC Magazines 2009
Book design © Woodlands Books 2009
All photographs © BBC Magazines 2009
All recipes contained within this book first
appeared in BBC Good Food magazine

The Random House Group Limited
Reg. No. 954009

Addresses for companies within the
Random House Group can be found at
www.randomhouse.co.uk

A CIP catalogue record for this book is available
from the British Library.

The Random House Group Limited supports
The Forest Stewardship Council (FSC), the
leading international forest certification organization.
All our titles that are printed on Greenpeace
approved FSC certified paper carry the FSC logo.
Our paper procurement policy can be found at
www.rbooks.co.uk/environment

To buy books by your favourite authors and
register for offers visit www.rbooks.co.uk

Printed and bound by Firmengruppe APPL,
aprinta druck, Wemding, Germany
Colour origination by Dot Gradations Ltd, UK

Commissioning Editor: Muna Reyal
Project Editor: Joe Cottington
Designer: Annette Peppis
Production: Phil Spencer
Picture Researcher: Gabby Harrington

ISBN: 9781846077685

GoodFood

101 SPEEDY SUPPERS
TRIPLE-TESTED RECIPES

Editor
Jane Hornby

Contents

Introduction

Here at *Good Food* we're experts in creating delicious recipes for busy people – recipes that are quick to shop for, easy to follow and work first time.

There can never be too many ways to feed a family in a hurry, so look no further than *101 Speedy Suppers* for new weeknight meal ideas: here are tasty, economical suppers for two, four or more that are sure to get the thumbs up.

There's no need to spend hours in the kitchen when you're entertaining; choose a starter and main from 'Speedy but special', and a dessert from 'Quick and easy puds', to impress your guests without the stress. Or, if you're really against the clock, check out the 'Superfast' section: a whole chapter of meals and snacks that are ready in just 15 minutes or less, and that are so much fresher than a takeaway. If you're concerned about what you eat but don't have time to worry about it, there's a whole array of healthy recipes to choose from as well, for both veggie and non-veggie alike.

Keep *101 Speedy Suppers* to hand and that 'what's for dinner' dilemma will be a thing of the past. Welcome to quick and scrumptious home cooking.

Jane

Jane Hornby
Good Food magazine

Notes and conversion tables

NOTES ON THE RECIPES

• Eggs are large in the UK and Australia and extra large in America unless stated otherwise.

• Wash fresh produce before preparation.

• Recipes contain nutritional analyses for 'sugar', which means the total sugar content including all natural sugars in the ingredients, unless otherwise stated.

OVEN TEMPERATURES

Gas	°C	°C Fan	°F	Oven temp.
¼	110	90	225	Very cool
½	120	100	250	Very cool
1	140	120	275	Cool or slow
2	150	130	300	Cool or slow
3	160	140	325	Warm
4	180	160	350	Moderate
5	190	170	375	Moderately hot
6	200	180	400	Fairly hot
7	220	200	425	Hot
8	230	210	450	Very hot
9	240	220	475	Very hot

APPROXIMATE WEIGHT CONVERSIONS

• All the recipes in this book list both imperial and metric measurements. Conversions are approximate and have been rounded up or down. Follow one set of measurements only; do not mix the two.

• Cup measurements, which are used by cooks in Australia and America, have not been listed here as they vary from ingredient to ingredient. Kitchen scales should be used to measure dry/solid ingredients.

Good Food are concerned about sustainable sourcing and animal welfare so where possible, we use organic ingredients, humanely-reared meats, free-range chickens and eggs and unrefined sugar.

SPOON MEASURES

Spoon measurements are level unless otherwise specified.

- 1 teaspoon (tsp) = 5ml
- 1 tablespoon (tbsp) = 15ml
- 1 Australian tablespoon = 20ml (cooks in Australia should measure 3 teaspoons where 1 tablespoon is specified in a recipe)

APPROXIMATE LIQUID CONVERSIONS

metric	imperial	AUS	US
50ml	2fl oz	¼ cup	¼ cup
125ml	4fl oz	½ cup	½ cup
175ml	6fl oz	¾ cup	¾ cup
225ml	8fl oz	1 cup	1 cup
300ml	10fl oz/½ pint	½ pint	1¼ cups
450ml	16fl oz	2 cups	2 cups/1 pint
600ml	20fl oz/1 pint	1 pint	2½ cups
1 litre	35fl oz/1¾ pints	1¾ pints	1 quart

With just 5 ingredients and 15 minutes you can make a memorable pasta dish that's smart enough for weeknight entertaining.

Lemon and parsley spaghetti with prawns

175g/6oz spaghetti
2 tbsp olive oil
140g/5oz large raw peeled prawns, thawed if frozen
zest and juice of 1 lemon, plus wedges to serve (optional)
1 small bunch of flatleaf parsley, roughly chopped

Takes 15 minutes • Serves 2

1 Cook the pasta according to the packet instructions.
2 Meanwhile, heat the oil in a large pan, add the prawns, then quickly fry until they are evenly pink.
3 Drain the spaghetti, reserving two tablespoons of the cooking water.
4 Add the lemon zest and juice, parsley, two tablespoons of cooking water and salt and pepper to the prawns, then heat through.
5 Toss the pasta together with the prawns. Serve with lemon wedges, if liked.

• Per serving 455 kcalories, protein 23g, carbohydrate 65g, fat 13g, saturated fat 2g, fibre 3g, sugar 3g, salt 0.37g

A hearty slice of cheese on toast ticks all the boxes when time is short – satisfying, quick to make and popular with everyone.

Chillied cheese on toast

4 slices from a ciabatta loaf (cut on an angle to make the slices larger)
1 bunch of spring onions, finoly oliood
100g/4oz cherry tomatoes, quartered
100g/4oz Gruyère, grated (or use Cheddar)
1 tsp dried chilli flakes
a splash of Worcestershire sauce

Takes 10 minutes • Serves 4

1 Heat the grill to high, put the bread on to a baking sheet, then grill until just golden on both sides.
2 Mix together the onions, tomatoes, cheese and chilli flakes in a bowl, then spread over the toast. Shake over a little Worcestershire sauce and grill again until golden and melted.

Per serving 230 kcalories, protein 13g, carbohydrate 28g, fat 11g, saturated fat 6g, fibre 2g, sugar 3g, salt 1.16g

To make this even quicker you could easily use ready-cooked tandoori chicken.

Crunchy coronation chicken salad

2 skinless chicken breasts
1 tsp mild or medium curry powder
3 tbsp olive oil
2 tbsp mango chutney
½ lemon
½ cucumber, sliced into sticks
50g/2oz watercress
2 tbsp toasted flaked almonds

Takes 15 minutes • Serves 2

1 Slice the chicken breasts across the middle, but not quite all the way, then open them out – this will make them cook quicker. Rub the chicken with the curry powder and one tablespoon of the oil. Heat a large non-stick pan and cook the chicken for 4 minutes on each side or until golden and cooked through. Cut into strips.
2 In a large bowl, whisk together the remaining oil and mango chutney with a good squeeze of lemon juice. Toss in the cucumber, watercress, chicken strips and most of the flaked almonds.
3 Divide between two bowls, scatter with the rest of the almonds, and enjoy with some crusty bread on the side, if you like.

• Per serving 399 kcalories, protein 37g, carbohydrate 10g, fat 24g, saturated fat 3g, fibre 2g, sugar 9g, salt 0.78g

A satisfying bowl of home-made soup can be ready in no time;
it's economical and tastes so much better than bought.

Minty pea and potato soup

800g/1lb 12oz potatoes, peeled and
cut into big chunks
2 tsp vegetable oil
1 onion, chopped
1 litre/1¾ pints vegetable stock
350g/12oz frozen peas
a handful of fresh mint leaves,
chopped
fresh bread, to serve

Takes 15 minutes • Serves 4

1 Put the potatoes into a food processor
and chop roughly. Heat the oil in a large pan,
then fry the onion for 5 minutes until softened.
Add the potatoes and stock, then bring to the
boil. Cover and simmer for 5–7 minutes until
tender, adding the peas 2 minutes before the
end of the cooking time.
2 Use a slotted spoon to remove a quarter
of the vegetables from the pan and set aside.
Blend the remaining vegetables and stock in
the food processor or using a hand blender
until smooth, then stir through the reserved
veg, chopped mint and some seasoning.
Serve with bread on the side.

• Per serving 249 kcalories, protein 11g, carbohydrate
48g, fat 3g, saturated fat 1g, fibre 9g, sugar 7g,
salt 0.36g

This open-sandwich version of the classic French croque-madame really hits the spot.

Open breakfast sandwich

8 chunky slices country-style bread
50g/2oz softened butter
3 tbsp mayonnaise
8 slices smoked ham
100g/4oz Cheddar, grated
2 tomatoes, sliced thickly
1 tbsp sunflower oil
4 large eggs
1 tbsp chopped fresh parsley
(optional)

Takes 15 minutes • Serves 4

1 Heat the grill to medium. Place the bread on a large baking sheet, spread one side with butter then grill, butter side up, for 2 minutes until golden. Turn over, spread with the mayonnaise, then top with the ham, cheese and tomatoes. Grill for 3–4 minutes until the cheese has melted and the edges of the bread are golden.
2 Meanwhile, heat the oil in a large non-stick frying pan and fry the eggs for 3 minutes, covering the pan with a lid for the last minute to set the yolks.
3 Divide the ham and cheese toasts among four plates and top each toast with an egg. Scatter over some parsley, if using, and season to taste.

• Per serving 661 kcalories, protein 29g, carbohydrate 48g, fat 41g, saturated fat 17g, fibre 4g, sugar 3g, salt 3.14g

Frozen broad beans are small and tender, so there's no need to pop them out of their shells for this creamy and delicate pasta.

Chicken and broad bean tagliatelle

4 skinless chicken breasts
1 tsp olive oil
300g/10oz tagliatelle
175g/6oz frozen broad beans
85g/3oz reduced-fat crème fraîche
juice of 1 lemon
6 tbsp finely grated Parmesan,
a small handful of fresh parsley,
chopped

Takes 15 minutes • Serves 4

1 Heat the grill to high. Put the chicken on to a baking sheet, coat with the oil, season, then grill for about 12 minutes, turning halfway through the cooking time.

2 Meanwhile, cook the pasta according to the packet instructions, adding the beans for the final 3 minutes, then drain, reserving 150ml/¼ pint of the cooking water.

3 Slice the cooked chicken and put it into the pasta pan with the crème fraîche, lemon juice, the reserved cooking water and four tablespoons of the Parmesan. Heat gently, season to taste, then stir in the parsley and pasta. Serve sprinkled with the remaining Parmesan.

• Per serving 524 kcalories, protein 50g, carbohydrate 62g, fat 10g, saturated fat 5g, fibre 5g, sugar 2g, salt 0.47g

A few storecupboard deli ingredients will perk up a panini or pizza base in no time. Also good with fresh tomatoes, ham and mushrooms – in fact, whatever you have in the fridge.

Pepper and tuna panini pizzas

4 panini rolls
280g jar roasted peppers, drained
1 tbsp tomato purée
a small handful of fresh parsley, chopped
200g can tuna, drained
125g ball mozzarella, torn into small pieces

Takes 15 minutes • Serves 4

1 Heat the grill to medium. Split the panini rolls in half and lightly toast each of them on both sides.
2 Cut the peppers into strips and mix well with the tomato purée, parsley and some seasoning. Spread over the toasted bread.
3 Flake the tuna over the pepper mixture, then scatter with the cheese. Grill for 3–5 minutes until the cheese is golden and bubbling.

• Per serving 393 kcalories, protein 25g, carbohydrate 38g, fat 17g, saturated fat 7g, fibre 3g, sugar 3g, salt 2.37g

We've turned a classic starter into a filling yet healthy main-meal option that requires no cooking whatsoever.

Prawn cocktail salad

FOR THE SALAD
200g bag large cooked prawns
1 large ripe avocado, halved, peeled and sliced
200g punnet cherry tomatoes, halved
4 spring onions, finely sliced
1 romaine lettuce, shredded
2 tbsp olive oil
juice of ½ lemon

FOR THE DRESSING
3 tbsp mayonnaise
2 tbsp ketchup
juice of ½ lemon

Takes 10 minutes • Serves 4

1 Whisk together the dressing ingredients. If it seems a little thick, add a splash of water.
2 Put the prawns, avocado, tomatoes, spring onions and lettuce in a large salad bowl, drizzle with the olive oil and lemon juice, toss gently, then serve with the dressing handed round separately.

• Per serving 297 kcalories, protein 14g, carbohydrate 6g, fat 25g, saturated fat 3g, fibre 3g, sugar 5g, salt 1.35g

The simple sauce for this dish can be made in the time it takes
to boil the pasta.

Two-step carbonara

350g/12oz spaghetti or linguine
140g pack diced pancetta
or chopped smoked
streaky bacon
2 tbsp olive oil
1 garlic clove, crushed
1 egg, plus 4 yolks
50g/2oz Parmesan, grated

Takes 15 minutes • Serves 4

1 Cook the pasta according to the packet instructions.

2 Meanwhile, fry the pancetta in the oil for a few minutes until golden and crisp. Add the garlic to the pan, fry for 1 minute, then turn off the heat. Briefly whisk the whole egg and yolks with most of the Parmesan and some seasoning.

3 Drain the pasta, reserving a little of the cooking water. Add the whisked egg and yolks and one tablespoon of cooking water to the pasta, then mix until the pasta is coated and creamy. The heat from the pasta will gently cook the eggs. Stir in the pancetta and garlic then serve, topped with the remaining Parmesan.

• Per serving 575 kcalories, protein 28g, carbohydrate 65g, fat 24g, saturated fat 9g, fibre 3g, sugar 3g, salt 2.11g

This classic Italian tuna sauce is savoury and piquant, and really livens up leftover turkey or chicken. Try it – you'll be surprised.

Turkey or chicken tonnato salad

100g/4oz mayonnaise (an olive-oil one works best)
1 tbsp capers, drained
2 anchovies from a can, 1 cut into thin slices
80g can tuna in oil (a good-quality one makes all the difference here), drained
juice of ½ lemon
about 400g/14oz leftover turkey or chicken (white and/or brown meat)
100g bag rocket leaves

Takes 10 minutes • Serves 4

1 Put the mayonnaise, most of the capers, the whole anchovy, the tuna and most of the lemon juice into a food processor. Whiz until the tuna is completely mixed into the mayo. Season with pepper first, then taste, and add salt and more lemon juice, if you need to. If your sauce seems a bit thick, whiz in a drop of water. This dressing can be made up to a day ahead and chilled until needed.
2 Spread the turkey or chicken and rocket over a large serving plate, then spoon over the dressing and scatter with the remaining capers and the sliced anchovy. Serve straight away with crusty bread, if you like.

• Per serving 263 kcalories, protein 33g, carbohydrate 1g, fat 14g, saturated fat 3g, fibre 1g, sugar 1g, salt 0.76g

A sophisticated French-style salad, ready in no time.

Baby spinach and bacon bistro salad

140g/5oz fine green beans
4 tbsp olive oil, plus an extra dash
6 rashers smoked streaky bacon, chopped
a good handful of ready-made croûtons
200g/8oz mushrooms, sliced
1 avocado, halved and sliced
250g/9oz baby leaf spinach

FOR THE DRESSING
1 small garlic clove, crushed
1 tbsp wholegrain mustard
1 tbsp red wine vinegar
3 tbsp extra-virgin olive oil

Takes 15 minutes • Serves 4

1 Boil the beans for 3 minutes until just cooked, drain in cold water, then drain again. Meanwhile, heat the oil in a large frying pan, then sizzle the bacon until crisp. Scoop the bacon into a large salad bowl.
2 Toss the croûtons in the bacon juices, then tip them in with the bacon. Tip a splash more oil into the pan, very briefly fry the mushrooms just to rid them of their rawness, then turn off the heat. When the mushrooms have cooled slightly, tip them into the salad bowl along with the beans and avocado.
3 Mix the dressing ingredients together with one tablespoon of water and season with salt and pepper. Moments before serving, add the spinach leaves and dressing, then toss really well so everything is coated.

• Per serving 395 kcalories, protein 10g, carbohydrate 13g, fat 34g, saturated fat 6g, fibre 4g, sugar 3g, salt 1.51g

Come home to a tasty and quick twist on eggs on toast.
This recipe is easily doubled.

Scrambled omelette toast topper

2 eggs
1 tbsp crème fraîche
25g/1oz Cheddar, grated
a small bunch of chives, snipped
(or use another spring onion)
1 tsp oil
1 spring onion, sliced
3–4 cherry tomatoes, halved
2 slices crusty bread, toasted

Takes 10 minutes • Serves 1

1 Beat together the eggs, crème fraîche, cheese and chives with a little seasoning.
2 Heat the oil in a pan, then soften the spring onion for a few minutes. Add the tomatoes and warm through, then pour in the egg mixture. Cook over a low heat, stirring, until the eggs are just set. Pile over the toasted bread and serve.

• Per serving 571 kcalories, protein 30g, carbohydrate 42g, fat 33g, saturated fat 13g, fibre 2g, sugar 4g, salt 1.98g

This easy egg-fried rice with extras will be a sure-fire favourite with kids and teenagers. Always make sure leftover rice is piping hot before you tuck in.

Fast-fix fried rice

2 tsp oil
1 egg, beaten
2 rashers bacon, chopped
175g/6oz mushrooms, sliced
200g/8oz frozen peas
1 garlic clove, crushed
a small knob of fresh root ginger, grated
2 tsp dark soy sauce, plus extra to serve (optional)
1 tsp sugar
250g/9oz cooked basmati rice (leftover or from a pouch)

Takes 10 minutes • Serves 2

1 Heat the oil in a frying pan, then tip in the egg. Leave to set for 30 seconds–1 minute, swirling every now and again, then tip it out and finely slice. Add the bacon and mushrooms to the pan, then fry until golden, about 3 minutes. Toss in the peas, garlic and ginger, then cook for 1 minute.

2 Mix the soy sauce and sugar together. Turn up the heat, add the cooked rice to the pan, heat through, then splash in the sweet soy sauce. Stir through the egg and serve straight away, with more soy sauce, if you like.

• Per serving 355 kcalories, protein 18g, carbohydrate 48g, fat 11g, saturated fat 3g, fibre 6g, sugar 6g, salt 1.81g

There's no excuse not to cook when you can get this ready in just 7 minutes. It's high in fibre and low in fat too – not many ready-made snacks can boast that!

Smoky bacon pot noodle for one

1 rasher smoked back bacon, trimmed of fat and chopped
2 spring onions, finely sliced (white and green parts kept separate)
50g/2oz frozen peas
¼ tsp paprika
2 tsp cornflour
200ml/7fl oz vegetable stock
150g block straight-to-wok wheat noodles
a splash of Worcestershire sauce

Takes 7 minutes • Serves 1 (easily doubled)

1 In a small non-stick pan, fry the bacon for a few minutes, add the white parts of the spring onions, the peas and paprika, then cook for 1 minute more.
2 Meanwhile, mix the cornflour with a little of the stock to get a paste, then stir this into the pan with the rest of the stock, the noodles and a good splash of Worcestershire sauce. Simmer for a couple of minutes until thick and saucy, then scatter with the green parts of the spring onions.

• Per serving 356 kcalories, protein 15g, carbohydrate 68g, fat 5g, saturated fat 1g, fibre 8g, sugar 4g, salt 1.29g

Another tasty filling idea for these tortillas is leftover roast chicken with grated cheese, mango chutney and chopped spring onions.

Salsa chicken and cheese tortillas

4 tbsp hot salsa, from a jar
2 large flour tortillas
215g can kidney beans, drained, rinsed and roughly mashed
1 spring onion, chopped
50g/2oz leftover roast chicken, shredded
85g/3oz grated mature Cheddar
½ × 20g pack coriander, leaves chopped (optional)
oil, for brushing

Takes 15 minutes • Serves 2

1 Spread two tablespoons of salsa on to each tortilla, then evenly top one of them with the beans, spring onion, chicken and Cheddar. Scatter with coriander, if you like. Sandwich with the other tortilla, then brush one side with oil.

2 Heat a large non-stick frying pan, then cook the tortilla, oil-side down, for 3 minutes. Carefully turn over with a palette knife (or by turning it out onto a plate, sliding it back into the pan), then cook for 2 minutes on the other side until golden. Serve cut into wedges.

• Per serving 533 kcalories, protein 27g, carbohydrate 44g, fat 29g, saturated fat 12g, fibre 6g, sugar 7g, salt 3.18g

These skewers taste better than any takeaway – and they're low fat too.

Oriental beef skewers with cucumber salad

4 thin-cut sirloin or minute steaks, trimmed of any fat and each cut into 3 long strips
120ml sachet stir-fry sauce (we used oyster & spring onion)
1 tbsp sesame seeds

FOR THE SALAD
1 tsp white wine vinegar
1 tsp light soy sauce
1 cucumber
3 spring onions, sliced
½ red chilli, seeded
a handful of fresh coriander leaves
basmati rice, to serve (optional)

Takes 15 minutes • Serves 4

1 Heat the grill to high. In a bowl, mix the steak strips with the stir-fry sauce and sesame seeds. Thread on to 12 skewers (pre-soak if wooden), then grill for 6 minutes, turning halfway through, until golden and a little sticky.

2 Meanwhile, prep the salad ingredients. Mix the vinegar and soy together. Cut the cucumber into chunks and chop the spring onions, chilli and coriander. Mix everything into the dressing. Serve with the beef skewers and some rice, if you like.

• Per serving 228 kcalories, protein 32g, carbohydrate 8g, fat 8g, saturated fat 3g, fibre 1g, sugar 8g, salt 2.21g

Look no further than your storecupboard for this filling, family-friendly dish.

Cheesy tuna pesto pasta

400g/14oz penne
200g can yellowfin tuna steaks in olive oil
190g jar basil pesto (or try a different flavour such as spinach, tomato or aubergine)
100g/4oz Cheddar, grated
250g punnet cherry tomatoes, halved
green salad, to serve

Takes 15 minutes • Serves 4

1 Cook the pasta according to the packet instructions.
2 Meanwhile, tip the tuna and its oil into a bowl with the pesto. Mash together with a wooden spoon. Stir in a third of the cheese and all of the tomatoes. Heat the grill to high
3 Drain the pasta, then toss with the pesto mix. Tip into a shallow baking dish, scatter with the remaining cheese, then grill for 3 minutes until just melted. Serve with a green salad.

• Per serving 696 kcalories, protein 40g, carbohydrate 79g, fat 27g, saturated fat 11g, fibre 4g, sugar 5g, salt 1.5g

This is a classic spring salad that makes the most of the season's home-grown (and very quick-cooking) asparagus.

Tuna, asparagus and white bean salad

1 large bunch asparagus
1 red onion
2 × 200g cans yellowfin tuna steaks in water, drained
2 × 400g cans cannellini beans in water, drained and rinsed
2 tbsp capers
1 tbsp olive oil
1 tbsp red wine vinegar
2 tbsp fresh tarragon, finely chopped

Takes 15 minutes • Serves 4

1 Cook the asparagus in a large pan of boiling water for 4–5 minutes until tender. Drain well, cool under running water, then cut into finger-length pieces.
2 Meanwhile, finely chop the onion. Toss together the tuna, beans, onion, capers and asparagus in a large serving bowl.
3 Mix the oil, vinegar and tarragon together then pour over the salad and serve.

• Per serving 275 kcalories, protein 33g, carbohydrate 26g, fat 5g, saturated fat 1g, fibre 8g, sugar 6g, salt 1.28g

This is an ideal recipe for getting your Thai tastebuds into practice – serve with extra fresh lime juice, sugar and fish sauce on the side, so everyone can adjust their own flavourings.

Thai chicken and mushroom broth

1 litre/1¾ pints hot chicken stock
1 tbsp Thai red curry paste
1 tbsp Thai fish sauce
2 tsp sugar
zest and juice of 1 lime, plus extra to serve
100g/4oz portobello mushrooms, sliced
a bunch of spring onions, sliced (white and green parts kept separate)
200g/8oz leftover cooked chicken, shredded

Takes 15 minutes • Serves 4

1 Tip the stock into a pan, then stir in the curry paste, fish sauce, sugar, lime juice and most of the zest. Bring to the boil, then add the mushrooms and whites of the spring onions. Cover, then simmer for 2 minutes.
2 Stir in the chicken and most of the spring onion greens to heat through gently, then ladle into bowls and serve scattered with the remaining lime zest.

• Per serving 179 kcalories, protein 25g, carbohydrate 6g, fat 6g, saturated fat 1g, fibre 1g, sugar 4g, salt 2.32g

Pile flavoursome tomatoes on to warm, garlicky slices of toast spread with ricotta for a sophisticated snack so good that it could also be served as a summer starter or even a light lunch too.

Summertime bruschetta

4 tbsp extra-virgin olive oil
1 small garlic clove, crushed
8 slices sourdough or country-style bread
200g pot ricotta
12 fresh basil leaves, shredded, plus extra to serve
350g/12oz cherry tomatoes on the vine

Takes 15 minutes • Serves 4

1 Heat the grill to high. Pour the olive oil into a jug and stir in the garlic. Set aside.
2 Place the slices of bread on a large baking sheet and grill for 2 minutes on each side until golden. Remove and brush with a little of the garlicky oil.
3 Meanwhile, put the ricotta into a bowl and stir in the shredded basil. Halve some of the tomatoes and place in a bowl with two tablespoons of the garlicky oil.
4 Spread each slice of toast with a generous amount of basil ricotta, top with the whole tomatoes still on the vine, then spoon over the garlicky tomatoes. Season with salt and pepper, and finish with a drizzle more garlicky oil and a few basil leaves scattered over.

• Per serving 390 kcalories, protein 11g, carbohydrate 49g, fat 18g, saturated fat 5g, fibre 4g, sugar 5g, salt 1.07g

This recipe is easily doubled to serve four if you have plenty of leftover chicken; if you have less, bump up the protein with a handful of cashew nuts.

Tasty chicken noodles

2 blocks medium egg noodles
2 tsp cornflour
2 tbsp fish or soy sauce
1 tbsp sugar
1 tbsp sunflower oil
1 large red pepper, seeded and chopped
2 garlic cloves, thinly sliced
4 spring onions, sliced
200g/8oz leftover roast chicken, shredded
1 tsp ground coriander
½ tsp chilli powder
100g/4oz frozen peas
½ × 20g pack fresh basil or coriander, leaves roughly shredded

Takes 15 minutes • Serves 2
(easily doubled)

1 Cook the noodles according to the packet instructions.
2 Meanwhile, mix the cornflour with the fish or soy sauce and sugar until smooth, then add eight tablespoons of water.
3 Heat the oil in a wok, then stir-fry the pepper, garlic and spring onions for about 3 minutes. Tip in the chicken, spices and peas, stir-fry for a couple of seconds more, then pour in the fish/soy sauce and cornflour mix. Stir until thickened, then toss in the drained noodles and shredded basil or coriander.

• Per serving 820 kcalories, protein 48g, carbohydrate 114g, fat 22g, saturated fat 5g, fibre 8g, sugar 18g, salt 4.95g

Try adding a few olives to this tasty pasta dish, which makes a perfect Italian-style family supper.

Sausage, mushroom and tomato pasta

400g/14oz penne
1 tbsp sunflower or olive oil
454g pack good-quality sausages, cut into chunky pieces
250g pack chestnut mushrooms, halved
500g pack cherry tomatoes
2 fresh rosemary sprigs, leaves roughly chopped
a handful of flatleaf parsley, chopped

Takes 20 minutes • Serves 4

1 Cook the pasta according to the packet instructions.
2 Meanwhile, heat the oil in a deep frying pan, then fry the sausages and mushrooms for 5 minutes until golden. Add the tomatoes and cook for about another 3 minutes on a high heat until the tomatoes pop and start to form a sauce.
3 Season to taste, add the herbs and drained pasta, then stir well to combine.

• Per serving 681 kcalories, protein 29g, carbohydrate 86g, fat 27g, saturated fat 7g, fibre 5g, sugar 8g, salt 1.52g

Stir-frying good steak can be a waste as it's hard to control its cooking. This twist on a classic lets you cook it the way you like it.

Five-spice beef with black bean sauce and bok choi

2 tsp Chinese five spice powder
1 large sirloin steak (about 300g/10oz)
3 bok choi heads, halved
1 tsp sesame oil
steamed rice, to serve

FOR THE SAUCE
100g sachet black bean sauce
2 garlic cloves, finely crushed
1 small knob fresh root ginger, grated
2 tbsp rice wine vinegar

Takes 30 minutes • Serves 2

1 Mix the sauce ingredients together in a small pan, then gently simmer until hot.
2 Heat a griddle pan until very hot. Rub the five-spice all over the steak, then season with a little salt and pepper. Sear the steak for around 2–3 minutes on each side for medium–rare (or until cooked to your liking), then leave to rest.
3 Meanwhile, gently simmer or steam the bok choi for 4–5 minutes until wilted, but still crunchy. Toss the greens in a few tablespoons of the sauce and the sesame oil.
4 Cut the steak into thick slices. Serve on a plate with a small pot of the remaining sauce, plus the greens and some steamed rice.

• Per serving 352 kcalories, protein 36g, carbohydrate 13g, fat 18g, saturated fat 7g, fibre 3g, sugar 9g, salt 4.50g

Here is a fishcake with a difference. To make a quick raita, mix a 150g
pot of natural yogurt with a teaspoon of mint jelly and a tablespoon of
chopped fresh coriander, then season to taste.

Indian-spiced fish cakes

600g/1lb 5oz potatoes, cut into
cubes
½ tsp cumin seeds
2 spring onions, finely chopped
1 red chilli, seeded and finely
chopped
2 tbsp chopped fresh coriander
1 egg, beaten
100g/4oz cooked leftover salmon,
flaked into large pieces
plain flour, for coating
25g/1oz butter
1 tbsp sunflower oil
raita (see recipe in intro) or mango
chutney and salad leaves,
to serve

Takes 30 minutes • Serves 2

1 Boil the potatoes in a pan of lightly salted
water for 10–15 minutes until tender.
2 Meanwhile, dry-fry the cumin seeds for
a couple of seconds in a large non-stick
frying pan.
3 When soft, drain the potatoes, return them
to the pan, then add the cumin, onions,
chilli and coriander with plenty of seasoning.
Mash well. When cooled a little, beat in two
tablespoons of the egg, then carefully stir
through the salmon. Shape into four rough
cakes, then coat in flour.
4 In the frying pan, melt the butter with the
oil. Fry the cakes for about 2 minutes each
side until golden. Serve with the raita or some
mango chutney and salad leaves.

• Per serving 551 kcalories, protein 23g, carbohydrate
60g, fat 26g, saturated fat 9g, fibre 4g, sugar 2g,
salt 0.43g

Lemon chicken is easy to make at home with a few storecupboard
ingredients and tastes a lot fresher than a takeaway.

Lemon chicken with spring veg noodles

1 tbsp sunflower oil
2 skinless chicken breasts, cut into
strips
zest and juice of 1 lemon
1 tbsp caster sugar
2 tsp grated fresh root ginger
2 tsp cornflour
125g pack or 2 blocks medium
egg noodles
200g/8oz frozen pea and bean mix
4 spring onions, sliced
1 tbsp roasted cashew nuts

Takes 20 minutes • Serves 2

1 Heat the oil in a non-stick pan, then fry the
chicken for 5 minutes until almost cooked
through. Tip out onto a plate. Pour 225ml/
8fl oz of water into the pan with the lemon
zest and juice, sugar and ginger.
2 In a bowl, mix the cornflour with a little
water until smooth, then whisk into the
pan. Bring to the boil, stirring, then add the
chicken to the sauce. Reduce the heat.
Bubble for a few minutes until the chicken is
cooked and the sauce thickened.
3 Meanwhile, cook the noodles and veg
together in boiling water for 4 minutes, then
drain. Toss together the chicken, noodles,
veg and spring onions. Serve in individual
bowls scattered with cashews.

• Per serving 553 kcalories, protein 47g, carbohydrate
69g, fat 12g, saturated fat 2g, fibre 6g, sugar 12g,
salt 1.10g

Give lamb and potatoes a bit of zing with lemony, garlicky
houmous, herbs and olives.

Lamb steaks with houmous
new potatoes

500g/1lb 2oz new potatoes
2 lamb leg steaks
1 tsp olive oil
1 bunch of cherry tomatoes on
the vine
3 tbsp houmous
10 pitted green olives, roughly
chopped
a small handful of flatleaf parsley,
chopped

Takes 20 minutes • Serves 2

1 Cook the potatoes in boiling salted water
for 15 minutes or until tender.
2 After 5 minutes, heat the grill or a griddle
pan. Season the lamb steaks, rub with a little
oil, then griddle or grill for 3–4 minutes on
each side until they are cooked to your liking,
adding the tomatoes halfway through and
cooking them until juicy and bursting.
3 When the potatoes are ready, drain well,
then return to the pan and gently crush with
a fork or potato masher. Stir through the
houmous, olives and parsley, then season
well. Serve the crushed potatoes with the
lamb and the tomatoes.

• Per serving 552 kcalories, protein 46g, carbohydrate
43g, fat 23g, saturated fat 7g, fibre 5g, sugar 5g,
salt 1.70g

Gnocchi make a great, and very quick-cooking, alternative to pasta in any recipe. This hearty mince dish is a good way to get kids to eat their spinach.

Gnocchi bolognese with spinach

500g/1lb 2oz lean minced beef
1 tsp olive oil
2 × 400g cans chopped tomatoes
1 tbsp dried Italian herbs
500g/1lb 2oz gnocchi
400g/14oz fresh spinach, washed
125g ball reduced-fat mozzarella

Takes 30 minutes • Serves 4

1 Fry the mince in the oil for a few minutes. Tip in the tomatoes and herbs. Fill one of the empty cans with water, add this to the beef, then bring to the boil. Simmer for 20 minutes.
2 When the bolognese is almost ready, cook the gnocchi according to the packet instructions. Lift from the pan with a spoon.
3 Tip half the spinach into a colander then pour some of the boiling gnocchi cooking water over it to wilt it, then repeat with the second half. Squeeze out as much moisture from the spinach as you can, then leave to drain in the colander. Heat the grill to high.
4 Stir the gnocchi and spinach into the bolognese sauce, season, then tip into a large ovenproof dish. Tear the mozzarella into pieces, scatter over, then grill until golden and bubbling.

• Per serving 518 kcalories, protein 44g, carbohydrate 50g, fat 18g, saturated fat 8g, fibre 6g, sugar 8g, salt 2.40g

Finger food at its best, this quick and spicy supper has three of your 5-a-day. The spicy fish makes an easy and tasty change to bought crumbed-fish pieces.

Curried fish tacos with bean salad

1 ripe avocado, peeled and chopped
juice of ½ lemon
½ × 410g can kidney beans, drained
and rinsed
1 finger-length piece of cucumber,
diced
85g/3oz cherry tomatoes, halved
2 skinless haddock fillets (each about
110g/5oz)
1 tbsp plain flour
1 tbsp mild curry powder
2 tsp vegetable oil
4 taco shells, soured cream and lime
wedges, to serve

Takes 15 minutes • Serves 2

1 Mix the avocado with the lemon juice in a bowl. Add the beans, cucumber and tomatoes, then mix well with some seasoning. Set aside.
2 Slice the fish into thick finger-length strips and toss in a bowl with the flour and curry powder.
3 Heat the oil in a large non-stick pan, then fry the fish slices for 1 minute on each side until cooked through. Serve in the tacos, with the bean salad, soured cream and lime wedges.

• Per serving 396 kcalories, protein 35g, carbohydrate 23g, fat 19g, saturated fat 2g, fibre 9g, sugar 5g, salt 1g

Bought pizza bases can be real life-savers; keep one in the freezer ready to load up to make this delicious dish. Perfect with a crisp salad.

Sausage and tomato pizza

1 tbsp olive oil
1 large red onion, peeled and finely sliced
2 garlic cloves, crushed
5 tbsp passata
a pinch of sugar
1 large (25cm) pizza base
2 sausages, cut into thin slices
50g/0 ▪▪ grated cheese (any kind)
a handful of fresh basil leaves, to scatter

Takes 20 minutes • Serves 2

1 Preheat the oven to 220°C/200°C fan/gas 7. Heat the olive oil in a pan and fry the onion and garlic until softened, about 5 minutes.

2 Season the passata with a pinch of sugar and some salt and pepper.

3 Put the pizza base on to a baking sheet and spread over the passata, leaving a border around the edge. Top with the onions, sausages and, finally, the cheese. Bake in the oven for 10 minutes until crisp.

4 Scatter with basil just before serving.

• Per serving 654 kcalories, protein 26g, carbohydrate 75g, fat 30g, saturated fat 11g, fibre 4g, sugar 11g, salt 3g

You can use dried lentils for this recipe if you have more time; simply boil 200g/8oz lentils in plenty of water for 20 minutes until tender, then drain and rinse.

Garlic prawns with Asian puy lentils

2 red chillies, seeded and finely chopped
zest and juice of 1 lime
2 large garlic cloves, crushed
2 tbsp oil
400g/14oz raw peeled tiger prawns, defrosted if frozen
2 × 250g packs ready-cooked Puy lentils

FOR THE DRESSING
2 tbsp soy sauce
1 tbsp clear honey
1 tbsp rice wine vinegar
3 tbsp sesame seeds, toasted
a bunch of fresh coriander, leaves roughly chopped

Takes 25 minutes • Serves 4

1 Mix together half the chopped chillies, lime zest and juice, garlic and oil, then pour it over the prawns in a shallow dish. Cover and chill for 15 minutes to marinate.
2 To make the dressing, put the remaining chopped chillies, the soy, honey and vinegar into a small bowl and stir together.
3 Heat the lentils according to the packet instructions, then tip them into a bowl. Spoon over almost all the dressing while the lentils are hot, tip in the sesame seeds, then mix well.
4 Heat a frying pan. Lift the prawns out of the marinade, then fry for 1–2 minutes each side until pink and lightly golden. Pour the marinade into the pan and bring to the boil.
5 Fold the chopped coriander through the lentils, then spoon on to serving plates. Top with the prawns and any pan juices.

• Per serving 349 kcalories, protein 33g, carbohydrate 29g, fat 12g, saturated fat 2g, fibre 5g, sugar 4g, salt 1.89g

No need to wait until Sunday for your roast – this satisfying meal can be rustled up in just half an hour.

Quick roast lamb

400g/14oz new potatoes
250g/9oz Chantenay carrots or large carrots cut into big chunks
1 tbsp oil, plus a little more for the lamb
1 fresh rosemary sprig, leaves chopped
100ml/3½fl oz red wine
100ml/3½fl oz lamb stock (from a cube is fine)
1–2 tsp redcurrant jelly
4 lamb chops or cutlets
green beans or other veg, to serve

Takes 30 minutes • Serves 2

1 Preheat the oven to 220°C/200°C fan/gas 7. Put the potatoes and carrots on to a baking sheet, toss with the oil and rosemary, then season well. Roast for 15 minutes on the top shelf until the veg is golden and almost tender.
2 Meanwhile, make the gravy. Put the wine and stock into a small pan, then boil until reduced by about two-thirds. Stir in the redcurrant jelly, season and keep warm.
3 Rub the lamb in a little oil, then season. Tuck the lamb in among the veg, then return to the oven for 8–10 minutes, turning the lamb halfway through. Serve with the redcurrant gravy and some green veg.

• Per serving 606 kcalories, protein 34g, carbohydrate 44g, fat 32g, saturated fat 13g, fibre 5g, sugar 13g, salt 0.70g

Soya beans make a fresh and fast alternative to mashed potatoes in this pretty, light main meal for two.

Lemon cod with basil bean mash

2 small bunches cherry tomatoes on the vine
1 tbsp olive oil
2 × 140g/5oz chunks skinless cod or other white fish fillet
zest of 1 lemon, plus juice of ½
½ × 480g pack frozen soya beans
1 garlic clove
a bunch of fresh basil, leaves and stalks separated
100ml/3½fl oz chicken or vegetable stock

Takes 25 minutes • Serves 2

1 Preheat the oven to 200°C/180°C fan/gas 6. Put the tomatoes on to a baking sheet, rub with a little oil and some seasoning, then roast for 5 minutes until the skins are starting to split. Add the fish to the baking sheet, top with most of the lemon zest, some more seasoning and a little more oil. Roast for 8–10 minutes until the fish flakes easily.
2 Meanwhile, cook the beans in a pan of boiling water for 3 minutes until just tender. Drain, then tip into a food processor with the rest of the oil, the garlic, basil stalks, lemon juice and stock, then pulse to a thick, slightly rough purée. Season to taste.
3 Divide the tomatoes and bean mash between two plates, top with the fish, then scatter with the basil leaves and the remaining lemon zest to serve.

• Per serving 372 kcalories, protein 44g, carbohydrate 17g, fat 15g, saturated fat 3g, fibre 6g, sugar 3g, salt 0.50g

Serve this classic Chinese pork with rice and green vegetables,
or sliced thinly to top a big bowl of soup noodles.

Sticky pork with spring onions

4 pork steaks, left whole
1 bunch of spring onions

FOR THE MARINADE
2 tbsp rice wine (or use dry sherry)
6 tbsp dark soy sauce
2 garlic cloves, crushed
4 tsp light muscovado sugar

Takes 30 minutes • Serves 4

1 Put the marinade ingredients into a large freezer bag, add the pork and shake to coat. Leave for 20 minutes (or, if you have more time, overnight in the fridge). Meanwhile, shred the onions.
2 Heat the grill to medium and put the steaks on to the grill pan, reserving a little of the marinade. Cook until sticky and glazed, about 8 minutes, turning over halfway through cooking and spooning over a little more of the marinade every now and then.
3 Once the meat is done, rest it on a plate while you finish the sticky glaze. Put the remaining marinade into a small pan and boil for a few seconds until syrupy. Slice the pork, spoon over the reduced marinade and sprinkle with the spring onions to serve.

• Per serving 365 kcalories, protein 30g, carbohydrate 10g, fat 23g, saturated fat 9g, fibre 1g, sugar 9g, salt 4.28g

Keep the washing-up down to an absolute minimum with this one-pot supper – you can even eat it out of the cooking dish!

One-pot chicken pilaf

1 tsp sunflower oil
1 small onion, chopped
1 large or 2 small skinless chicken thigh fillets, cut into chunks
2 tsp curry paste (choose your favourite)
85g/3oz basmati rice
200ml/7fl oz chicken stock
140g/5oz mixed frozen veg
a handful of frozen leaf spinach

Takes 25 minutes • Serves 1 (easily doubled)

1 Heat the oil in a heavy-based frying pan, then fry the onion for 5–6 minutes until softened. Add the chicken pieces, fry for a further couple of minutes just to colour the outside, then stir in the curry paste and rice. Cook for another minute.
2 Pour in the chicken stock and throw in any larger bits of frozen veg. Bring to the boil, lower the heat, then cover the pan with a lid. Cook for 10 minutes, then stir in the remaining veg. Scatter over the spinach, cover, then cook for 10 minutes more until all the stock is absorbed and the rice is tender. Give everything a good stir, season to taste, then tuck in.

• Per serving 663 kcalories, protein 50g, carbohydrate 92g, fat 13g, saturated fat 2g, fibre 10g, sugar 13g, salt 1.94g

All the flavour of meatballs, but with a fraction of the fat.

Herbed turkey meatballs

85g/3oz breadcrumbs
75ml/2½fl oz milk
350g/12oz minced turkey
2 tsp dried oregano
a small bunch of flatleaf parsley,
chopped
2 tsp olive oil
680g bottle of onion and garlic
passata
4 tsp sugar
500g bag pasta shapes

Takes 30 minutes • Serves 5

1 Tip the breadcrumbs into a large bowl, then stir in the milk until they have absorbed the liquid. Add the mince, half the oregano and half the parsley, then season and mix with a fork. Using wet hands, shape the mixture into 30 meatballs.
2 Heat the oil in a large non-stick pan, then brown the meatballs for 5 minutes, turning to cook all over. Pour in the passata, sugar, remaining oregano and most of the remaining parsley. Stir, then simmer for 8–10 minutes until the meatballs are cooked through.
3 Meanwhile, cook the pasta according to the packet instructions. Drain the pasta and tip into a serving bowl. Season the sauce, spoon the meatballs and sauce over the pasta, then sprinkle over any remaining parsley.

• Per serving 260 kcalories, protein 25g, carbohydrate 33g, fat 4g, saturated fat 1g, fibre 1g, sugar 12g, salt 1.45g

Use up your leftovers in this comforting family recipe. To make it vegetarian, stir wilted spinach and crumbled blue cheese through instead of ham.

Creamy ham and mushroom pasta bake

500g bag farfalle or other pasta shape
50g/2oz butter, plus 1 tsp
200g/8oz small mushrooms, halved
a bunch of spring onions, finely sliced
50g/2oz plain flour
500ml/18fl oz milk
140g/5oz thickly cut ham, chopped
140g/5oz mature Cheddar, grated

Takes 30 minutes • Serves 5

1 Cook the pasta according to the packet instructions, then drain. Preheat the oven to 200°C/180°C fan/gas 6.
2 Melt the teaspoon of butter in a large pan. Fry the mushrooms for a couple of minutes, then scoop out and set aside. Use some kitchen paper to wipe out the pan.
3 Melt the remaining butter in the pan, then add most of the onions and soften for 1 minute. Stir in the flour for another minute, then gradually stir in the milk. Increase the heat and bubble the sauce, stirring for a few minutes to thicken. Turn off the heat, stir in the ham and most of the cheese, and season.
4 Tip the pasta and mushrooms into an ovenproof dish, then pour over the sauce and mix well. Scatter over the remaining cheese and spring onions, then bake for 10 minutes.

• Per serving 678 kcalories, protein 31g, carbohydrate 89g, fat 25g, saturated fat 14g, fibre 4g, sugar 8g, salt 1.58g

Create your own bistro-style salad – full of flavour and just perfect
with crusty bread.

Warm new potato salad with bacon and blue cheese

500g/1lb 2oz new or salad potatoes,
thickly sliced
2 tbsp olivo oil
2 red onions, each sliced into
6 wedges
4 rashers smoked back bacon,
trimmed and cut into large pieces
140g/5oz mushrooms, sliced
1 tbsp wholegrain mustard
1 tbsp red wine vinegar
100g bag mixed watercress and
spinach salad
85g/3oz creamy blue cheese,
to garnish

Takes 30 minutes • Serves 4

1 Preheat the oven to 220°C/200°C fan/
gas 7. Place the potatoes in a roasting tin,
then rub with a tablespoon of the oil and
sprinkle with salt. Roast for 15 minutes, then
add the onion wedges to the tin. Roast for
15 minutes more until the potatoes have turned
golden brown and the onions started to soften.
Remove from the oven and leave to cool.
2 Meanwhile, heat a non-stick frying pan. Fry
the bacon without adding any extra fat, then
add the mushrooms and cook for 5 minutes.
3 Whisk together the mustard, vinegar and
remaining tablespoon of oil with a splash of
water to make a dressing.
4 Put the potatoes, onions, bacon,
mushrooms and salad leaves in a bowl, pour
over the dressing, then toss well. Crumble
over the blue cheese and serve.

• Per serving 289 kcalories, protein 11g, carbohydrate
25g, fat 17g, saturated fat 7g, fibre 3g, sugar 5g,
salt 1.65g

Kids will just love the sweet, sticky crunchiness of this quick meal that's also simple to shop for.

Sticky ribs with corn salad

12 small or 8 large pork ribs
150ml/¼ pint barbecue sauce
340g can sweetcorn, drained
and rinsed
½ cucumber, diced
1 red chilli, seeded and finely
chopped
½ red onion, chopped
1 lime, half juiced, half cut into
wedges, to serve

Takes 30 minutes • Serves 4

1 Heat the grill. In a large pan of water, simmer the ribs for 15 minutes. Drain and pat dry. In a large roasting tin, toss the ribs with the barbecue sauce, then grill for 8–10 minutes, turning halfway, until the ribs are sticky.
2 Mix the corn, cucumber, chilli, onion and lime juice in a large bowl with some seasoning.
3 Just before serving, shake the tin so the ribs are evenly coated in sauce. Divide the ribs among four plates and serve with the corn salad and lime wedges.

• Per serving 449 kcalories, protein 34g, carbohydrate 30g, fat 22g, saturated fat 8g, fibre 2g, sugar 18g, salt 1.22g

Don't wait until summer to enjoy a nice niçoise – sundried tomatoes pack in the flavour when fresh aren't at their best.

Winter tuna niçoise

450g/1lb waxy potatoes, unpeeled and thickly sliced
2 tbsp olive oil, plus 2 tsp for roasting
4 eggs
1 tbsp red wine vinegar
2 tbsp capers, rinsed
50g/2oz sundried tomatoes in oil, finely chopped
½ red onion, thinly sliced
100g/4oz baby leaf spinach
2 × 160g or 200g cans yellowfin tuna steak in spring water, drained

Takes 30 minutes • Serves 4

1 Preheat the oven to 200°C/180°C fan/gas 6. Toss the potatoes in the two teaspoons of oil and add some seasoning. Tip on to a large baking sheet, then roast for 20 minutes, stirring halfway, until crisp, golden and cooked through.

2 Meanwhile, put the eggs in a small pan of water, bring to the boil, then simmer for 8-10 minutes, depending on how you like them cooked. Plunge into a bowl of cold water to cool for a few minutes. Peel away the shells, then halve.

3 In a large salad bowl, whisk together the remaining oil, the red wine vinegar, capers and chopped tomatoes. Season, tip in the onion, spinach, tuna and potatoes, then gently toss together. Top with the eggs, then serve straight away.

• Per serving 332 kcalories, protein 25g, carbohydrate 23g, fat 16g, saturated fat 3g, fibre 3g, sugar 3g, salt 1.35g

Rice is nice, but garlic bread is better! Our quick chilli con carne bake
is sure to become one of your favourite ways with mince.

Chilli and garlic bread bake

500g pack lean minced beef
2 onions, quartered
2 tsp olive oil
2 tsp ground cumin
1–2 tsp mild chilli powder (or hotter if
you like it spicy)
400g can chopped tomatoes
1 beef stock cube
1 garlic baguette, split into slices

Takes 30 minutes • Serves 4

1 Brown the mince in a large non-stick frying
pan for a few minutes, then tip into a bowl.
Whiz the onions in a food processor until
finely chopped (or roughly grate them if you
don't have a processor).
2 Heat the oil in the pan then fry the onions
for 2 minutes. Add the spices and cook for
another minute. Return the mince to the pan
with the tomatoes, stock cube and a can of
hot water, bring to the boil then simmer
for 20 minutes.
3 Heat the grill to medium. Spoon the mince
into an ovenproof dish. Arrange the baguette
slices over the mince, then grill for 5 minutes
until golden and crisp.

• Per serving 498 kcalories, protein 37g, carbohydrate
33g, fat 25g, saturated fat 6g, fibre 2g, sugar 7g,
salt 2.16g

Roasted peppers, olives and paprika give this pie tons of flavour.
It's a great way to use up leftover cooked chicken too.

Spanish chicken pie

1kg/2lb 4oz potatoes, cut into small cubes
3 tsp paprika (use smoked paprika if you have it)
2 onions
2 garlic cloves
2 tsp olive oil
2 × 400g cans chopped tomatoes
300g/10oz leftover cooked chicken, shredded
140g roasted peppers from a jar, sliced
a handful of Kalamata olives, pitted and halved

Takes 30 minutes • Serves 4

1 Preheat the oven to 200°C/180°C fan/gas 6. Boil the potatoes for 10–15 minutes until tender. Drain, return to the pan, then mash with some seasoning and two teaspoons of the paprika.
2 Meanwhile, slice the onions and crush the garlic. Heat the oil in a large pan, then fry them together for a few minutes until softened. Stir in the remaining paprika for 1 minute, add the tomatoes, then bring to a simmer. Tip into a large ovenproof dish, then stir in the chicken, peppers, olives and some seasoning.
3 Spoon the mash over the chicken then bake for 15 minutes until the mash is golden on top and the sauce is bubbling.

• Per serving 421 kcalories, protein 30g, carbohydrate 57g, fat 10g, saturated fat 2g, fibre 8g, sugar 10g, salt 1.32g

If you can't find ras-el-hanout, stir together equal parts of ground mixed spice, coriander and paprika, then add a pinch of cayenne and black pepper to give this dish its characteristic Moroccan flavour.

Spice and honey salmon with couscous

zest and juice of 1 lemon, plus 1 lemon cut into wedges to serve
2 tsp ras-el-hanout spice mix
1 large or 2 small garlic cloves, crushed
a bunch of spring onions, thinly sliced
3 tsp olive oil, plus extra for drizzling
2 skinless salmon fillets
140g/5oz couscous
2 tsp clear honey
a handful of fresh mint, leaves finely sliced

Takes 30 minutes • Serves 2 (easily doubled)

1 Preheat the oven to 200°C/180°C fan/gas 6. Mix the lemon zest and half the juice with the spice mix, garlic, half the spring onions and two teaspoons of the oil. Season well. Put the salmon into a shallow dish and cover with this mixture for 10 minutes.

2 Meanwhile, put the couscous in a large bowl. Tip in the remaining lemon juice and oil, spring onions and 150ml/¼ pint boiling water, then cover and leave to stand.

3 Lift the salmon on to a foil-lined baking sheet, spoon over any leftover marinade, then roast in the oven for 15 minutes. With 5 minutes to go, pull out the sheet and spoon a teaspoon of honey over each fillet.

4 Fork the mint through the couscous, then serve with the salmon and lemon wedges. Spoon over the juices from the baking sheet.

• Per serving 506 kcalories, protein 34g, carbohydrate 47g, fat 22g, saturated fat 4g, fibre 1g, sugar 8g, salt 0.21g

The economical and comforting family favourite that will really take you back to your childhood.

Must-make tuna pasta bake

600g/1lb 5oz any tube-shaped pasta
50g/2oz butter
50g/2oz plain flour
600ml/1 pint milk
340g can sweetcorn, drained and rinsed
2 × 160g cans yellow fin tuna steak in springwater, drained
250g/9oz strong Cheddar, grated
a large handful of fresh chopped parsley

Takes 25 minutes • Serves 6

1 Boil the pasta for 2 minutes less time than stated on the packet.
2 To make the sauce, melt the butter in a pan. Whisk in the flour and milk, and keep whisking until it comes to the boil and thickens. Stir in the sweetcorn and tuna until warmed through, then take off the heat and stir in all but a handful of the cheese.
3 Heat the grill to medium. Drain the pasta, mix with the sauce and parsley, then season. Transfer to a baking dish and top with the rest of the cheese. Grill for 5 minutes or until the cheese on top is golden and starting to brown.

• Per serving 752 kcalories, protein 37g, carbohydrate 99g, fat 26g, saturated fat 15g, fibre 4g, sugar 12g, salt 1.43g

Try this next time you want something fast, fresh and full of flavour.

Asparagus pasta with mint pesto

1 large bunch of fresh mint (about 85g/3oz), leaves stripped
250g tub ricotta
25g/1oz Parmesan, grated, plus extra to serve
400g/14oz farfalle (or other pasta shapes)
200g/8oz asparagus tips

Takes 15 minutes • Serves 4

1 In a food processor, briefly whiz the mint leaves, ricotta and Parmesan until you have a smooth green pesto. Season well.
2 Cook the pasta according to the packet instructions, dropping in the asparagus tips 2–3 minutes before the cooking time is up. When you drain the pasta, reserve a cup of the cooking water, then return the pasta, asparagus and a couple of tablespoons of water to the pan. Quickly stir in the mint pesto, adding more water if it seems at all dry, then divide among four plates. Shave over the remaining Parmesan to serve.

• Per serving 507 kcalories, protein 24g, carbohydrate 79g, fat 13g, saturated fat 7g, fibre 4g, sugar 5g, salt 0.43g

No fresh basil? Simply stir a couple of teaspoons of pesto into the pan before adding the eggs.

One-pan summer eggs

1 tbsp olive oil
400g/14oz courgettes (about 2 large), chopped into small chunks
200g pack cherry tomatoes, halved
1 garlic clove, crushed
2 eggs
a few fresh basil leaves, to garnish
crusty bread, to serve

Takes 20 minutes • Serves 2 (easily doubled)

1 Heat the oil in a non-stick frying pan, then add the courgettes. Fry for 5 minutes, stirring every so often until they start to soften. Add the tomatoes and garlic, then cook for a few minutes more.

2 Stir in a little seasoning, then make two gaps in the mix and crack in the eggs. Cover the pan with a lid or a sheet of foil, then cook for 2–3 minutes until the eggs are done to your liking. Scatter over a few basil leaves and serve with crusty bread.

• Per serving 196 kcalories, protein 12g, carbohydrate 7g, fat 13g, saturated fat 3g, fibre 3g, sugar 6g, salt 0.25g

You won't miss the meat in this hearty pasta.

Squash, mushroom and sage pasta

1 tbsp olive oil
½ butternut squash, peeled and
cubed (about 300g/10oz peeled
weight)
2 garlic cloves, chopped
a few fresh sage leaves, roughly
chopped
140g/5oz mushrooms, sliced
175g/6oz pasta, any shape
1 tbsp grated Parmesan, plus more
to serve, if you like

Takes 30 minutes • Serves 2

1 Heat the oil in a non-stick frying pan, then fry the squash, garlic and sage for a few minutes until beginning to brown. Splash in some water, then cook fiercely for about 15 minutes until the squash is softening and the pan looks dry. Add the mushrooms, then fry for 5 minutes more, stirring every so often, until everything begins to caramelize.
2 Meanwhile, cook the pasta according to the packet instructions. Drain, reserving a little of the cooking water, then add the pasta and reserved water to the squash. Toss with most of the Parmesan and serve in bowls, sprinkled with the remaining cheese.

• Per serving 441 kcalories, protein 15g, carbohydrate 80g, fat 9g, saturated fat 2g, fibre 6g, sugar 9g, salt 0.13g

Not only filling and different, but superhealthy too!

Pumpkin, spinach and black bean dopiaza

2 onions, thinly sliced
2 tbsp sunflower oil
1 garlic clove, crushed
1 tsp each ground cumin, ground coriander and curry powder
a pinch of chilli powder
400g/14oz pumpkin (peeled weight), cut into chunks
1 tbsp tomato purée
400g can black beans in water, drained and rinsed
200g/8oz fresh spinach, washed

Takes 30 minutes • Serves 2

1 Preheat the oven to 190°C/170°C fan/gas 5. Toss half the onions in a tablespoon of oil, then roast on a baking sheet for 15–20 minutes, until they are crisp and golden. Set aside.
2 Meanwhile, in a frying pan, fry the rest of the onions in the remaining oil until golden. Add the garlic and spices, cook for 1 minute. Add the pumpkin, tomato purée and 425ml/¾ pint boiling water, then return to the boil. Simmer, covered, for 15 minutes, then stir in the beans. Cook for a further 5 minutes.
3 Put the spinach in a colander and pour over a kettle of boiling water until it is wilted. Press with a wooden spoon to remove excess water, then roughly chop. Stir into the curry, then warm through. Serve scattered with the crisp roasted onions.

• Per serving 354 kcalories, protein 17g, carbohydrate 42g, fat 14g, saturated fat 2g, fibre 13g, sugar 14g, salt 0.51g

Try using noodles in a new way and top your salads with an irresistible crunch.

Spiced sweet potato salad with crisp noodles

2 medium sweet potatoes, peeled and cut into chunks
1 tsp cumin seeds
2 tsp sunflower oil, plus extra for frying
25g/1oz dried fine egg noodles
zest and juice of ½ orange
2 tsp red wine vinegar
2 handfuls of baby leaf spinach
1 avocado, peeled and sliced
½ red onion, finely sliced

Takes 25 minutes • Serves 2

1 Preheat the oven to 200°C/180°C fan/gas 6. Toss the potato chunks with the cumin, a teaspoon of the oil and some seasoning. Spread over a baking sheet, then roast for 20–25 minutes until tender and golden.
2 Meanwhile, cook the noodles according to the packet instructions, then drain. Heat 1cm of oil in a wok or deep pan. Fry the noodles in a couple of batches for 30 seconds until crisp. Remove with a slotted spoon, then drain well on kitchen paper.
3 When the potatoes are ready, whisk together the remaining oil with the orange zest and juice, red wine vinegar and a little seasoning. Tip the potatoes into a bowl with the spinach, avocado and red onion and drizzle with the dressing. Divide between two plates and crumble over the crispy noodles.

• Per serving 411 kcalories, protein 7g, carbohydrate 47g, fat 23g, saturated fat 3g, fibre 8g, sugar 13g, salt 0.41g

Ricotta is a mild cheese, so if you like your pizza to have a cheesier kick, sprinkle a good grating of Parmesan over the top.

Ricotta and basil pizza bread

1 onion, finely chopped
2 yellow peppers, seeded and roughly chopped
1 tsp olive oil
2 × 400g cans chopped tomatoes
500g bag mixed grain or granary bread mix
plain flour, for dusting
10 cherry tomatoes, halved or whole
250g tub ricotta
a few fresh basil leaves, to garnish

Takes 30 minutes • Serves 6

1 Preheat the oven to 220°C/200°C fan/gas 7. Soften the onion and peppers in the oil in a large pan for a few minutes. Pour in the tomatoes, season, then simmer for 10 minutes.

2 Meanwhile, make up the bread mix according to the packet instructions, then bring the dough together and knead a couple of times. Flour a large baking sheet and roll out the dough into a rectangle roughly 25cm x 35cm. Bake for 5 minutes on a shelf at the top of the oven until firm.

3 Remove from the oven, spread with the sauce, then add the cherry tomatoes and dollop over spoonfuls of the ricotta. Bake for 10 minutes more until the base is golden and crisp. Scatter with basil and serve straight away with a green salad, if you like.

• Per serving 291 kcalories, protein 14g, carbohydrate 41g, fat 9g, saturated fat 4g, fibre 9g, sugar 9g, salt 1.23g

Fresh, light and perfect for a warm summer's evening.

Halloumi, watermelon and mint salad

250g pack halloumi, thinly sliced
flesh from 1kg/2lb 4oz chunk
watermelon, sliced
200g pack fine green beans
1 small bunch of fresh mint, finely
shredded
juice of 1 lemon
1 tbsp olive oil, plus extra to drizzle
toasted pitta breads, to serve

Takes 15 minutes • Serves 4

1 Heat the grill to high. Lay the cheese on a baking sheet in a single layer, then grill for 2 minutes on each side until golden.
2 Toss the watermelon, beans and mint together with the lemon juice and olive oil, season well, then layer on plates with the slices of halloumi. Drizzle with a little more oil, if you like, then serve with warm toasted pittas.

• Per serving 287 kcalories, protein 14g, carbohydrate 12g, fat 20g, saturated fat 10g, fibre 1g, sugar 12g, salt 2.29g

Serve this as a light veggie supper with crusty bread, or as a side dish for grilled chicken or fish. Romano peppers are particularly sweet, but regular peppers will work just as well.

Baked and stuffed Romano peppers

2 Romano peppers, halved
and seeded
2 tbsp olive oil, plus 1 tsp
for roasting
1 slice wholegrain bread
2 tbsp pine nuts
2 tbsp grated Parmesan
1 red or green chilli, seeded
and chopped
2 tsp capers
a good handful of fresh parsley,
roughly chopped
200g/8oz baby leaf spinach

Takes 30 minutes • Serves 4

1 Preheat the oven to 190°C/170°C fan/gas 5. Put the peppers on a large baking tray, then drizzle with the teaspoon of oil and season. Bake for 20 minutes.
2 Meanwhile, toast the bread, then blitz into rough crumbs in a food processor. Mix with the pine nuts, Parmesan, chilli, capers, parsley, and remaining oil. Boil the kettle. Put the spinach in a colander, then pour over the boiling water to wilt the leaves. Press out as much liquid as possible.
3 Divide the spinach among the peppers, then top with the crumbs. Return to the oven for 15 minutes, then serve.

• Per serving 241 kcalories, protein 6g, carbohydrate 9g, fat 21g, saturated fat 3g, fibre 4g, sugar 8g, salt 0.60g

You could make these even quicker by mashing up leftover potatoes and veg from your Sunday roast.

Pea pakora pockets

500g/1lb 2oz floury potatoes, cut into small chunks
200g/8oz frozen peas
4–5 tsp curry powder (choose your favourite)
200g/7oz natural yogurt
1 small bunch of fresh mint, half roughly chopped
6 white or wholemeal pittas, halved
½ iceberg lettuce
½ red onion

Takes 30 minutes • Serves 4

1 Preheat the oven to 220°C/200°C fan/gas 7. Boil the potatoes in a pan for about 8 minutes, throwing in the peas for the final few minutes. Drain well, spoon out and reserve a few spoonfuls of peas, then return the rest to the pan. Add the curry powder and some seasoning, then mash together over a low heat. Stir in the reserved peas.
2 Using two tablespoons, shape the mix into rough rugby-ball shapes (you should get about 16), then place on a baking sheet lined with baking parchment. Bake for 15 minutes until golden and crisp around the edges.
3 Meanwhile, mix the yogurt with the chopped mint. Warm the halved pittas. Shred the lettuce and slice the onion, then toss with the remaining mint leaves. Serve the pakoras with all the extras for stuffing into pittas.

• Per serving 377 kcalories, protein 18g, carbohydrate 74g, fat 4g, saturated fat 1g, fibre 11g, sugar 10g, salt 1.24g

Veggie burgers can be a little dry sometimes, but not these, with two zingy toppings and creamy avocado.

Mexican bean burgers with lime yogurt and salsa

2 × 400g cans kidney beans, drained and rinsed
100g/4oz breadcrumbs
2 tsp mild chilli powder
1 small bunch of fresh coriander, stalks and leaves chopped
1 egg
200g tub fresh salsa
150g pot low-fat natural yogurt
juice of ½ lime
6 wholemeal buns, sliced
salad leaves, avocado and red onion slices, to serve

Takes 20 minutes • Makes 6 burgers

1 Heat the grill to high. Tip the beans into a large bowl, then roughly crush with a potato masher. Add the breadcrumbs, chilli powder, coriander stalks and half the leaves, the egg and two tablespoons of the salsa, season to taste, then mix together well with a fork.

2 Divide the mixture into six, then wet your hands and shape into burgers. Place on a non-stick baking sheet, then grill for around 4–5 minutes on each side until the burgers are golden and crisp.

3 While the burgers are cooking, mix the remaining coriander leaves with the yogurt, lime juice and a grind of black pepper. Split the buns in half and spread the bases with the yogurt mix. Top each with salad leaves, avocado, onion, a burger, another dollop of the lime yogurt and some salsa, then serve.

• Per serving 195 kcalories, protein 11g, carbohydrate 33g, fat 3g, saturated fat none, fibre 6g, sugar 7g, salt 1.38g

Mascarpone makes a great cheat's sauce for gnocchi and pasta.

Gnocchi with creamy tomato and spinach sauce

1 tbsp olive oil
2 garlic cloves, crushed
400g can chopped tomatoes
140g/5oz mascarpone
500g pack gnocchi
200g bag baby leaf spinach
a handful of fresh basil leaves and some Parmesan shavings, to garnish (optional)

Takes 20 minutes • Serves 4

1 Heat the oil in a frying pan. Fry the garlic until golden, then add the tomatoes. Season, then simmer for 10 minutes. Stir in the mascarpone, then cook for 2 minutes more.
2 Meanwhile, cook the gnocchi according to the packet instructions. Add the spinach for the final minute of cooking. Drain well, tip back into the pan, then stir the tomato and mascarpone sauce through. Mix well and serve immediately with the basil leaves and Parmesan shavings scattered over, if you like.

• Per serving 393 kcalories, protein 9g, carbohydrate 48g, fat 20g, saturated fat 11g, fibre 4g, sugar 7g, salt 1.67g

There's so much flavour and texture in this colourful salad, why not make double and enjoy it next day in your lunchbox too.

Spiced veg with lemony bulgar wheat salad

2 tbsp vegetable oil
2 tbsp clear honey
2 tsp harissa paste
2 small aubergines, cut into wedges
1 red pepper, seeded and cut into chunks
140g/5oz bulgar wheat
zest and juice of ½ lemon
a large handful of fresh mint leaves, chopped
Greek yogurt, to drizzle

Takes 30 minutes • Serves 2

1 Mix together the oil, honey and harissa, then drizzle half over the aubergines and pepper. Season well. Heat a griddle pan, then cook the veg for 10 15 minutes, turning until lightly charred and cooked through.
2 Meanwhile, tip the bulgar wheat into a large bowl and pour over boiling water so it is well covered. Let it sit, covered, for 10 minutes until softened and plump, then drain, pour over the remaining dressing, the lemon zest and juice and mint leaves. Season well and toss everything together. Serve the roasted vegetables on top of the bulgar, drizzled with Greek yogurt.

• Per serving 448 kcalories, protein 10g, carbohydrate 75g, fat 14g, saturated fat 2g, fibre 5g, sugar 21g, salt 0.12g

Vary this dish by flavouring the simple tomato sauce with whatever you have to hand – curry powder, pesto or fresh herbs.

Spicy tomato baked eggs

1 tbsp olive oil
2 red onions, chopped
1 red chilli, seeded and finely chopped
1 garlic clove, sliced
1 small bunch of fresh coriander, stalks and leaves chopped separately
2 × 400g cans cherry tomatoes
1 tsp caster sugar
4 eggs
crusty bread, to serve

Takes 25 minutes • Serves 2 (easily doubled)

1 Heat the oil in a frying pan that has a lid, then soften the onions, chilli, garlic and coriander stalks for 5 minutes until soft. Stir in the tomatoes and sugar, then bubble for 8–10 minutes until thick.

2 Using the back of a large spoon, make four dips in the sauce, then crack an egg into each one. Put a lid on the pan, then cook over a low heat for 6–8 minutes, until the eggs are done to your liking. Scatter with the coriander leaves and serve with crusty bread.

• Per serving 340 kcalories, protein 21g, carbohydrate 21g, fat 20g, saturated fat 5g, fibre 6g, sugar 17g, salt 1.25g

This is a brilliant starter – all you need to do is assemble everything.
For a change, try pecorino or feta instead of mozzarella.

Crisp prosciutto, pea and mozzarella salad with mint vinaigrette

4 slices prosciutto
100g/4oz peas, fresh or frozen
1 ball buffalo mozzarella (about
125g/4½oz), torn into large pieces

FOR THE VINAIGRETTE
juice of ½ orange
1 tbsp olive oil
a small handful of fresh mint, leaves
finely chopped, plus extra small
leaves to garnish

Takes 25 minutes • Serves 2

1 Heat a frying pan. Without adding any oil, fry the prosciutto slices until wrinkled and crisp. Place on a sheet of kitchen paper, leave to cool, break into large shards, then set aside.
2 Boil the peas in a pan of salted water for 2 minutes until just tender. Meanwhile, mix all the vinaigrette ingredients together, season, then set aside. (If making ahead, do not add the chopped mint until ready to serve, as it will discolour.) When the peas are cooked, drain, then run them under cold water until completely cool. Pat dry with kitchen paper.
3 To serve, divide the mozzarella between two plates, scatter the peas over and sit the prosciutto shards on top. Drizzle the dressing over, and scatter with the mint leaves.

• Per serving 372 kcalories, protein 25g, carbohydrate 11g, fat 26g, saturated fat 12g, fibre 5g, sugar 4g, salt 2.23g

Watercress makes a wonderful pesto that complements steak perfectly. This is delicious served with smooth garlic mash.

Griddled rump steak with watercress, hazelnut and red chilli pesto

50g/2oz blanched hazelnuts, toasted
1 red chilli, seeded and roughly sliced
85g/3oz watercress
1½ tbsp olive oil, plus extra for griddling
1 tbsp balsamic vinegar, plus 2 tsp
2 rump steaks (about 140g/5oz each)

Takes 30 minutes • Serves 2

1 Preheat the oven to 180°C/160°C fan/gas 4. Finely blend the nuts, chilli, 50g/2oz of the watercress, the olive oil, balsamic vinegar and some seasoning in a food processor to make the pesto. Set aside.

2 Heat a griddle pan until smoking hot. Rub the steaks with a little of the extra oil, then season both sides with salt. Cook the steaks on the griddle for 2 minutes on each side, this will give you medium–rare (cook for 3 minutes for medium or 4 for well done, if you prefer). Remove from the griddle and leave to rest on a plate for 5 minutes. Stir any juices from the resting steak into the pesto – they're delicious and shouldn't be wasted.

3 Serve the steak with the pesto, a drizzle of the extra balsamic and the remaining watercress to give a peppery bite.

• Per serving 475 kcalories, protein 37g, carbohydrate 4g, fat 35g, saturated fat 7g, fibre 2g, sugar 4g, salt 0.24g

A little asparagus goes a long way in this seasonal supper dish.
Perfect for a Friday-night meal with friends.

Roasted asparagus, pancetta and cherry tomato pasta

400g/14oz penne
500g/1lb 2oz asparagus, each
spear trimmed and cut into 3
pieces
2 tbsp olive oil
6 slices pancetta, snipped into
pieces
200g/8oz cherry tomatoes, halved
a good handful of fresh basil
leaves, torn
grated Parmesan, to garnish

Takes 25 minutes • Serves 4

1 Preheat the oven to 200°C/180°C fan/
gas 6. Cook the pasta according to the
packet instructions.
2 Put the asparagus into a roasting tin,
then toss with the oil and pancetta. Roast
for 10 minutes until the pancetta starts to
crisp up, stir in the tomatoes, then cook for
5 minutes more
3 Drain the pasta, then add to the roasting
tin along with the torn basil leaves and
seasoning. Stir well until everything is
glistening, then serve in bowls, scattered
with grated Parmesan.

• Per serving 520 kcalories, protein 22g, carbohydrate
80g, fat 15g, saturated fat 4g, fibre 5g, sugar 6g,
salt 0.82g

This starter (or nibble with drinks) is based on the classic Scandinavian recipe for gravadlax, but it is a lot less fuss to prepare!

Scandi smoked salmon potatoes

about 16 salad or new potatoes – longer shaped ones work best (we used Pink Fir Apple)
2 × 150g packs smoked salmon slices (or about 16 slices)
1 lemon, for squeezing
a few fresh dill fronds
150ml pot soured cream

FOR THE SWEET MUSTARD SAUCE
1 tbsp Dijon mustard
1 tbsp caster sugar
6 tbsp olive oil (half extra-virgin, half mild)
2 tbsp white wine vinegar
½ × 20g bunch dill, leaves well chopped

Takes 30 minutes • Serves 6 (as a starter)

1 Boil the potatoes in their skins for around 15 minutes until tender, then drain and cool. Meanwhile, whisk all the sauce ingredients together, except the dill.

2 Cut each slice of salmon in half to make two long strips. Halve the potatoes slightly on a diagonal, then wrap a piece of smoked salmon around each piece and place on to a platter. (If you want to add salt, go easy, as the salmon is highly seasoned.) Scatter with a grinding of black pepper, a squeeze of lemon and a few dill fronds.

3 Give the sauce a quick whisk, add the chopped dill, season to taste, then pour into a dipping bowl. Scoop the soured cream into another dipping bowl. To eat, dip the potatoes into the cream, then spoon over a little sauce.

• Per serving 291 kcalories, protein 15g, carbohydrate 17g, fat 19g, saturated fat 5g, fibre 1g, sugar 5g, salt 2.63g

These taste fantastic from the griddle or, even better, the barbecue. Dress the salad ahead, adding the mint at the last minute, for a stress-free and summery supper outside.

Lamb cutlets with lentil and feta salad

300g/10oz frozen peas
2 × 410g cans green lentils, drained and rinsed
4 tbsp white wine vinegar
2 tbsp caster sugar
1 small bunch of fresh mint, roughly chopped
200g pack reduced-fat feta, crumbled
8 lamb cutlets
1 tsp olive oil

Takes 20 minutes • Serves 4

1 Cook the peas in boiling water for 3–4 minutes until just tender, then drain. Mix with the lentils, vinegar, sugar and mint, then crumble in the feta and season well.
2 Heat a griddle pan, brush the cutlets with a little oil and season. Cook in the hot pan for 4 minutes on each side until browned and the middle is pink
3 Divide the lentil and feta salad among four bowls, then top with a couple of the cutlets per person.

• Per serving 716 kcalories, protein 52g, carbohydrate 33g, fat 43g, saturated fat 22g, fibre 7g, sugar 12g, salt 3.38g

You'll love this as a change from the classic pear and blue cheese salad. Dip and spread the cheese, as you would pâté, and linger over it with a glass of good wine.

Roquefort toasts with peppered pears

2 just ripe pears, cored and cut into 8 pieces
1 tsp mild olive oil
¼ tsp peppercorns, crushed (we used a mix of colours)
85g/3oz Roquefort
5 tbsp double or whipping cream
2 handfuls of baby salad leaves
slices from sourdough loaf, halved and toasted just before serving

FOR THE DRESSING
1 tsp walnut oil
2 tsp mild olive oil
1½ tsp wine vinegar (red or white)
½ tsp clear honey

Takes 25 minutes • Serves 2
(easily doubled)

1 Heat a griddle pan until very hot, brush or toss the pears with a little oil, sprinkle with the crushed peppercorns, then griddle for 1–2 minutes on each side until nicely striped.
2 Put the Roquefort into a mixing bowl, break it up a little with a wooden spoon, then beat until almost smooth. Very softly whip the cream in a small bowl, then fold into the cheese, then spoon into two small ramekins or pots.
3 Whisk the dressing ingredients together with some seasoning, turn the salad leaves in the dressing a few times to coat, then serve with the toasted sourdough, griddled pears and the cheese.

• Per serving 644 kcalories, protein 14g, carbohydrate 57g, fat 42g, saturated fat 21g, fibre 6g, sugar 17g, salt 2.65g

Make your own restaurant-style sauce in just a few minutes.

Rump steak with quick mushroom and red wine sauce

1 tbsp sunflower oil
2 rump steaks (each about 200g/8oz)
140g/5oz mushrooms, quartered
2 fresh thyme sprigs, leaves removed
150ml/¼ pint red wine
1 tbsp butter

Takes 15 minutes • Serves 2

1 Heat a non-stick frying pan. Rub half the oil all over the steaks, season them on both sides, then fry for 2–3 minutes each side for medium–rare, or cook to your liking. Remove from the pan, then set aside to rest.
2 Add the remaining oil to the pan, tip in the mushrooms and thyme leaves, then fry for a couple of minutes until softened and golden. Pour in the wine and bubble until reduced and syrupy, then turn off the heat and stir in the butter. Season to taste.
3 Serve the steaks with the mushroom sauce poured over.

• Per serving 500 kcalories, protein 43g, carbohydrate 4g, fat 32g, saturated fat 13g, fibre 1g, sugar 4g, salt 0.42g

Sweet and juicy langoustines are made even more special with a dousing of herby nut butter.

Langoustines with hazelnut butter

10 Scottish langoustines (or use king prawns), heads removed, shelled, and tails left on
1 tbsp hazelnuts, toasted
25g/1oz butter
a few fresh parsley leaves, finely chopped
1 tsp olive oil

Takes 20 minutes • Serves 2

1 Thread the langoustines carefully on to ten pre-soaked wooded skewers and chill for up to a day.
2 For the butter, finely grate or chop half the hazelnuts (grating gives the nuttiest flavour), then roughly chop the rest. Tip into a small pan with the butter, parsley and a little seasoning, then set aside.
3 When ready to serve, melt the hazelnut butter in the pan. Heat a griddle pan or barbecue, then brush the langoustines with the olive oil. Griddle each skewer for 1–2 minutes, turning, until pink and cooked.
4 Pile the skewers on to a platter, pour half the hazelnut butter over the langoustines, then serve the rest in a small bowl on the side for dipping.

• Per serving 222 kcalories, protein 19g, carbohydrate 1g, fat 16g, saturated fat 7g, fibre 1g, sugar none, salt 0.70g

Don't overlook pork if you're entertaining – choose good free-range meat for a juicy, full-of-flavour supper that's ready in a flash.

Balsamic pork with olives

3 tbsp olive oil
3 tbsp balsamic vinegar
1 tsp Dijon mustard
2 garlic cloves, crushed
4 boneless pork loin chops
2 handfuls of green olives, pitted and halved
a large handful of fresh basil leaves, chopped
cooked pasta, to serve

Takes 20 minutes • Serves 4

1 Mix the oil with the vinegar, mustard and garlic. Score the meat on both sides, season, then put into a dish. Pour over the balsamic mixture and leave to marinate for 5 minutes.
2 Heat a griddle pan until very hot. Lift the pork from the marinade, scraping off any garlic, then cook for 4 minutes on each side, reserving the marinade. Remove the meat and keep warm. Pour the marinade into the pan with the olives, cook for 2 minutes, then stir in the basil. Pour any juices from the pork into the pan, drizzle the sauce over the pork and serve with pasta.

• Per serving 487 kcalories, protein 27g, carbohydrate 2g, fat 41g, saturated fat 13g, fibre 1g, sugar 2g, salt 0.51g

Make your own Thai banquet with this easy punchy pork
and fresh crisp salad.

Satay pork with crunchy apple salad

3 tbsp crunchy peanut butter
3 tbsp sweet chilli sauce
4 lean pork steaks
juice of 2 limes
1 tsp Thai fish sauce
a pinch of sugar
2 apples, cored and thinly sliced
a small bunch of coriander, leaves
roughly torn
½ × small bunch of mint, leaves
roughly torn
jasmine rice, to serve

Takes 20 minutes • Serves 4

1 Heat the grill to high. Mix the peanut butter and sweet chilli sauce together, then season with black pepper only (the peanut butter is salty enough). Arrange the pork on a baking sheet, brush the tops with half the nutty mixture, then grill for 3 minutes. Carefully turn the pork steaks over, brush with the remaining mixture, then grill for 3-4 minutes more until just cooked through.

2 Meanwhile, make the salad. Mix together the lime juice, fish sauce and sugar in a bowl. Stir in the apple slices so they are well coated in the dressing, then toss with the coriander and mint. Serve the crunchy apple salad alongside the pork steaks, with jasmine rice on the side.

• Per serving 310 kcalories, protein 36g, carbohydrate 15g, fat 12g, saturated fat 3g, fibre 2g, sugar 15g, salt 1.08g

These make a delicious lunch to share, or, put on smaller pieces of bread, a great pre-dinner nibble.

Lemony prawn bruschettas

200g/8oz raw peeled king prawns
4 slices from a baguette, sliced on an angle
1 tsp olive oil
2 garlic cloves, thinly sliced
1 large red chilli, seeded and sliced
juice of 1 lemon
1 small bunch of fresh coriander leaves chopped
2 large handfuls of rocket, to garnish

Takes 20 minutes • Serves 2

1 Butterfly the prawns first: slit them all along their length, taking care not to cut all the way through. Pull out any traces of black using the tip of your knife.

2 Toast the bread and keep warm. Heat the oil in a wok, then fry the garlic and chilli until sizzling. Turn up the heat, add the prawns, then cook until they turn pink. Remove from the heat, then add the lemon juice and coriander. Season, then serve piled on the toast with rocket leaves scattered on top.

• Per serving 294 kcalories, protein 26g, carbohydrate 38g, fat 5g, saturated fat 1g, fibre 3g, sugar 3g, salt 1.48g

Dinner guests won't be able to resist this dish. If you're more likely to want two chops each, double the marinade ingredients too.

Lamb chops with fruity couscous and mint

4 (or 8) lamb chops, cutlets or leg steaks, trimmed
2 tsp smoked paprika
1 red onion, finely chopped
3 tbsp red wine vinegar
3 tbsp olive oil
200g/8oz couscous
5 tbsp pine nuts, toasted
8 dates, stoned and finely chopped
zest and juice of 2 lemons
20g pack each fresh mint and flatleaf parsley, roughly chopped

Takes 20 minutes • Serves 4

1 Place the lamb in a bowl. Sprinkle over the paprika, half the onion, a tablespoon of the vinegar and half a tablespoon of oil. Season, then set aside.
2 To make the couscous, boil the kettle and tip the couscous into a heatproof bowl. Stir in the pine nuts, dates, lemon zest and half the juice. Pour over 140ml/4¼fl oz boiled water, cover, then leave to stand for 10 minutes.
3 Heat the grill to high. Lift the lamb out of its marinade, grill for 2–3 minutes on each side, then rest, wrapped in foil, for 10 minutes.
4 Stir half the chopped herbs and some seasoning into the couscous, then add the remaining lemon juice. Mix together the remaining herbs, red onion, vinegar, oil and seasoning to make a herby vinaigrette. Serve the lamb and couscous with the vinaigrette.

• Per serving 635 kcalories, protein 35g, carbohydrate 50g, fat 34g, saturated fat 11g, fibre 2g, sugar 23g, salt 0.23g

When the weather's good, keep cooking to a minimum. Combine crisp cooked fish with a salad and a dollop of rich garlicky mayonnaise.

Courgette and watercress salad with grilled fish and herbed aïoli

about 12 baby courgettes
olive oil, to coat and fry
4 thick fillets sustainable white fish, skin on
juice of ½ lemon
1 bunch of fresh mint, leaves picked
100g bag watercress (or use rocket)

FOR THE HERBED AÏOLI
200ml/7fl oz good-quality olive-oil mayonnaise
1 fat garlic clove, crushed
a handful of fresh mixed soft herbs (such as chives, parsley, mint and dill), chopped, plus extra picked leaves, to scatter
lemon juice, to taste

Takes 20 minutes • Serves 4

1 Heat a griddle pan. Rub the courgettes with a teaspoon of oil, season, then griddle until just soft. Set aside while you make the aïoli. Mix the mayonnaise, garlic and chopped herbs together, then season with the lemon juice to taste.

2 Season the fish. Heat a non-stick frying pan until very hot, add a teaspoon of oil, then fry the fish, skin side down, for 3 minutes until crisp. Turn and fry the fish for just 30 seconds–1 minute more until it is cooked all the way through.

3 Whisk a tablespoon of oil with the juice of half a lemon and season. Gently toss the courgettes, mint and watercress or rocket into the dressing. Pile on to plates, top with the fish plus a dollop of aïoli, then scatter with herbs.

• Per serving 594 kcalories, protein 35g, carbohydrate 2g, fat 49g, saturated fat 7g, fibre 1g, sugar 2g, salt 0.37g

Scallops love a bit of lemon and chilli, and are ready in a flash.
The perfect way to impress last-minute guests.

Seared scallops with leeks and lemon chilli butter

4 young (but not baby) leeks, trimmed
12 scallops, roes on or off
1 tbsp olive oil
lemon wedges, to serve

FOR THE BUTTER
250g pack butter, softened
1 red chilli, seeded and finely chopped
2 garlic cloves, crushed
zest of 2 lemons
1 bunch of fresh parsley, leaves chopped, plus extra to serve

Takes 20 minutes, plus freezing
Serves 4

1 Beat the butter ingredients together, spoon on to a large sheet of cling film, wrap tightly in a sausage shape, then freeze.
2 Set up a pan with a steamer or suspend a metal colander over a pan. Cut the leeks in half lengthways, then slice into long strips, about the thickness of tagliatelle. Cover, then steam for 6 minutes. Season, then set aside.
3 Dry the scallops and season them. Heat a heavy-based pan, then add the oil. Once hot, sizzle the scallops for 2 minutes until caramelized. Turn, fry for 1 minute more, then take the lemon and chilli butter from the freezer and add a good few slices to the pan off the heat, spooning it over the scallops.
4 Wind nests of leeks on to plates, top with three scallops each, spoon over the sauce, then serve with lemon and the extra parsley.

• Per serving 588 kcalories, protein 19g, carbohydrate 3g, fat 56g, saturated fat 33g, fibre 2g, sugar 2g, salt 1.47g

A timeless entertaining classic. If you usually serve stroganoff with rice, try this herby pasta – it works beautifully with the creamy sauce.

Beef stroganoff with herby pasta

1 tbsp butter
1 tbsp olive oil
400g/14oz rump steak, trimmed
and very thinly sliced
300g/10oz small button mushrooms
400g/14oz pappardelle
3 shallots, finely chopped
1 tbsp plain flour
300ml/½ pint beef stock
1 tbsp Dijon mustard
1 tbsp tomato purée
3 tbsp crème fraîche
½ × 20g pack flatleaf parsley,
chopped

Takes 30 minutes • Serves 4

1 In a large non-stick frying pan, melt half the butter with half the oil. Increase the heat, then season the beef and quickly sear it in batches until browned on both sides. Remove the meat and set aside. Repeat with the mushrooms, then set aside with the beef. Cook the pasta according to the packet instructions.

2 Add the remaining butter and oil to the pan and soften the shallots for a few minutes. Stir in the flour for 1 minute, then gradually stir in the stock. Bubble for 5 minutes until thickened, then stir in the mustard, purée, crème fraîche and seasoning. Bubble for 1 minute more, then return the beef and mushrooms to the pan.

3 Drain the pasta, toss with half the parsley, season, then serve with the creamy stroganoff, sprinkled with the remaining parsley.

• Per serving 614 kcalories, protein 38g, carbohydrate 81g, fat 18g, saturated fat 7g, fibre 4g, sugar 4g, salt 0.94g

Folding lemon juice, capers and chopped parsley through crème fraîche makes a quick, special sauce for salmon, trout and white fish.

Salmon and spinach with tartare cream

1 tsp vegetable or sunflower oil
2 skinless salmon fillets
250g bag fresh spinach
2 tbsp reduced-fat crème fraîche
juice of ½ lemon
1 tsp capers, drained
2 tbsp chopped flatleaf parsley
lemon wedges, to serve

Takes 15 minutes • Serves 2
(easily doubled)

1 Heat the oil in a pan. Season the salmon on both sides, then fry for 4 minutes each side until each fillet is golden and the flesh flakes easily. Leave to rest on a plate while you cook the spinach.

2 Tip the spinach leaves into the hot pan, season well, then cover and leave to wilt for 1 minute, stirring once or twice. Spoon the spinach on to plates, then top with the salmon fillets.

3 Gently heat the crème fraîche in the pan with the lemon juice, capers and parsley, then season to taste. Be careful not to let it boil. Spoon the sauce over the fish, then serve with lemon wedges.

• Per serving 321 kcalories, protein 32g, carbohydrate 3g, fat 20g, saturated fat 5g, fibre 3g, sugar 3g, salt 0.77g

Make a smart Indian-inspired supper using storecupboard ingredients and some easy-to-cook duck breasts.

Fragrant duck breasts with wild rice pilaf

2 duck breasts, skin on
1½ tsp garam masala
1 tsp grated fresh root ginger
2 tbsp mango chutney, to serve

FOR THE PILAF
1 tbsp butter
1 tsp cumin seeds
100g/4oz mixed basmati and wild rice
300ml/½ pint chicken or vegetable stock
85g/3oz frozen peas
1 bunch of spring onions, finely sliced

Takes 30 minutes • Serves 2
(easily doubled)

1 Score criss-crossed lines into the duck skin, then rub in the garam masala and ginger.
2 Preheat the oven to 200°C/100°O fan/ gas 6. Heat a heavy, non-stick pan, then fry the duck, skin-side down, for 10 minutes until the fat runs out. Pour off the excess fat halfway through. Transfer to a roasting tin then roast, skin-side up, for 10 minutes, then leave to rest.
3 While the duck is cooking, melt the butter in a pan. Add the cumin seeds, fry for around 2–3 minutes, then stir in the rice for another few minutes. Pour over the stock, cover partly with a lid, then simmer for 10–12 minutes, adding the peas for the final 4 minutes. When the rice is cooked and all the liquid has been absorbed, fork through the spring onions and some seasoning to taste. Slice the duck and serve with the rice and a spoonful of chutney.

• Per serving 894 kcalories, protein 54g, carbohydrate 47g, fat 57g, saturated fat 17g, fibre 3g, sugar 3g, salt 1.37g

This is such a simple pasta sauce, but by using a few special ingredients it's transformed into a dish ideal for entertaining friends.

Hot-smoked salmon with creamy pasta and pine nuts

600g/1lb 5oz trofie or other pasta shape
100ml/3½fl oz white wine
142ml pot double cream
2 tbsp grated Parmesan
450g/1lb hot-smoked salmon, skin removed and flaked
85g/3oz toasted pine nuts, to
﬐﬙ﬖﬔﬕ

Takes 15 minutes • Serves 6

1 Cook the pasta according to the packet instructions.
2 Meanwhile, bring the wine to the boil in a large frying pan, then simmer for 1 minute. Reduce the heat, stir in the cream and season well.
3 When the pasta is cooked, drain briefly and tip into the frying pan with the sauce. Add the Parmesan and flaked salmon pieces, and gently mix together. Pile into bowls, sprinkle with pine nuts and serve.

• Per serving 702 kcalories, protein 33g, carbohydrate 78g, fat 30g, saturated fat 10g, fibre 3g, sugar 4g, salt 2.00g

Lose the fat, keep the flavour with this brilliant twist on curried chicken and rice.

Spiced chicken with rice and crisp red onions

2 skinless chicken breasts,
(each about 140g/5oz)
1 tbsp sunflower oil
2 tsp curry powder
1 large red onion, thinly sliced
100g/4oz basmati rice
1 cinnamon stick
a pinch of saffron strands
1 tbsp raisins
85g/3oz frozen peas
1 tbsp each chopped fresh mint and coriander leaves
4 rounded tbsp low-fat natural yogurt

Takes 30 minutes • Serves 2
(easily doubled)

1 Preheat the oven to 190°C/170°C fan/gas 5. Brush the chicken with one teaspoon of oil, then sprinkle with curry powder. Toss the onion in the remaining oil. Put the chicken and onions in one layer in a roasting tin. Bake for 25 minutes until the meat is cooked and the onions are crisp, stirring the onions halfway through the cooking time.

2 Meanwhile, rinse the rice, then put it in a pan with the cinnamon, saffron, salt to taste and 300ml/10fl oz water. Bring to the boil, stir once, add the raisins, cover. Gently cook for 10–12 minutes until the rice is tender, adding the peas halfway through.

3 Spoon the rice on to two plates, top with the chicken and scatter over the crispy onions. Stir the herbs into the yogurt and season, if you like, before serving on the side.

• Per serving 495 kcalories, protein 45g, carbohydrate 63g, fat 9g, saturated fat 2g, fibre 5g, sugar 15g, salt 0.39g

Mackerel is such great value and so good for you. Pair it with flavoursome chickpeas for a well-balanced, scrumptious meal.

Basil and lemon chickpeas with mackerel

3 tbsp olive oil, plus extra for drizzling
1 bunch of spring onions, sliced
1 large garlic clove, crushed
zest of 1 lemon and squeeze of juice
2 × 400g cans chickpeas, drained and rinsed
150ml/¼ pint vegetable stock
85g/2 oz sundried tomatoes in oil, halved
4 mackerel fillets, skin on
20g pack fresh basil, leaves torn

Takes 25 minutes • Serves 4

1 Heat two tablespoons of the oil in a large, shallow pan. Add the spring onions, garlic and lemon zest, then cook for 2 minutes until the onions are tender but still very green. Add the chickpeas, then stir until well coated in the onion mixture. Lightly crush with a potato masher, then add the stock and tomatoes. Simmer for 3–4 minutes or until the liquid is absorbed, then remove to cool slightly.
2 Meanwhile, heat the remaining oil in a non-stick frying pan over a medium heat. Season the mackerel and fry for 3 minutes each side, starting on the skin side.
3 Add the basil and a squeeze of lemon juice to the chickpeas, then season to taste. To serve, spoon the warm chickpeas on to serving plates, drizzle with a little extra olive oil and top with the mackerel fillets.

• Per serving 486 kcalories, protein 29g, carbohydrate 24g, fat 31g, saturated fat 5g, fibre 7g, sugar 4g, salt 1.21g

This Indian favourite is easy to prepare at home. The juicy skewers are grilled, too, so you get all the flavour without the calories.

Chicken tikka skewers with cucumber salad

150g pot low-fat natural yogurt
2 tbsp hot curry paste
4 skinless chicken breasts, cubed
250g pack cherry tomatoes
4 wholemeal chapatis, warmed, to serve

FOR THE CUCUMBER SALAD
½ cucumber, halved lengthways, seeded and sliced
1 red onion, thinly sliced
a handful of chopped fresh coriander leaves
juice of 1 lemon
50g pack lamb's lettuce or pea shoots

Takes 30 minutes, plus soaking and marinating (optional) • Serves 4

1 Put eight wooden skewers in a bowl of water to soak. Mix the yogurt and curry paste together in a bowl, then add the chicken (if you have time, marinate it for an hour or so).
2 In a large bowl, toss together the cucumber, red onion, coriander and lemon juice. Chill until ready to serve.
3 Shake off any excess marinade, then thread the chicken pieces and cherry tomatoes on to the skewers. Cook under a medium grill for 15–20 minutes, turning from time to time, until cooked through and nicely browned.
4 Stir the lettuce or pea shoots into the salad, then divide among four plates. Top each serving with two chicken tikka skewers and serve with the warm chapatis.

• Per serving 214 kcalories, protein 37g, carbohydrate 8g, fat 4g, saturated fat 1g, fibre 1g, sugar 7g, salt 0.61g

For a healthy take on meatballs, try this easy storecupboard recipe that the whole family will enjoy.

Italian tuna balls

2 × 160g cans tuna in sunflower
or olive oil, drained (reserve a
little oil)
a small handful of pine nuts
finely grated zest of 1 lemon
a small handful of fresh parsley
leaves, roughly chopped
50g/2oz fresh breadcrumbs
1 egg, beaten
400g/14oz spaghetti
500g jar tomato pasta sauce

Takes 20 minutes • Serves 4
(easily halved or doubled)

1 Flake the tuna into a bowl, then tip in the pine nuts, lemon zest, parsley, breadcrumbs and egg. Season and mix together with your hands until completely combined. Roll the mixture into 12 walnut-sized balls.

2 Put a large pan of salted water on to boil, then cook the spaghetti according to the packet instructions.

3 Heat the reserved tuna oil in a large non-stick frying pan, then fry the tuna balls for 5 minutes, turning every minute or so until completely golden. Drain on kitchen paper. Heat the tomato sauce, then toss together with the pasta and tuna balls.

• Per serving 594 kcalories, protein 35g, carbohydrate 92g, fat 12g, saturated fat 2g, fibre 4g, sugar 8g, salt 1.42g

If you think lentils are boring, here's a salad to change
your mind – it's superhealthy and supertasty.

Warm mushroom and lentil salad with goat's cheese

3 tbsp olive oil
250g/9oz chestnut mushrooms, sliced
2 tbsp red wine vinegar
2 tsp Dijon mustard
2 red peppers, seeded and finely chopped
½ red onion, finely chopped
400g can lentils, drained and rinsed
2–3 Little Gem lettuces, leaves separated
100g/4oz goat's cheese, crumbled to scatter

Takes 20 minutes • Serves 4

1 Heat two tablespoons of the oil in a non-stick frying pan, then quickly fry the mushrooms until just starting to soften. Remove from the heat, then stir in the remaining oil with the vinegar and mustard. Stir well until mixed, then add the peppers, onion and lentils, and mix well again.
2 Arrange the lettuce leaves over four plates. Spoon the lentil salad over the top, scatter over the goat's cheese and serve.

• Per serving 220 kcalories, protein 10g, carbohydrate 15g, fat 14g, saturated fat 4g, fibre 4g, sugar 7g, salt 1.31g

This salad is a good source of omega-3, iron and calcium, and counts as two of your 5-a-day.

Superhealthy salmon salad

100g/4oz couscous
1 tbsp olive oil, plus extra to drizzle
200g/8oz sprouting broccoli, roughly
shredded, larger stalks removed
2 skinless salmon fillets
juice of 1 lemon
seeds from ½ pomegranate
a small handful of pumpkin seeds
a handful of fresh watercress
lemon wedges, to serve

Takes 25 minutes • Serves 2

1 Heat some water in a tier steamer. Season the couscous, then toss with a teaspoon of the oil. Pour boiling water over the couscous so it covers it by 1cm, then set aside.

2 When the water in the steamer comes to the boil, tip the broccoli into the water, then lay the salmon in the tier above. Cook for 3 minutes until the salmon is cooked and the broccoli tender. Drain the broccoli and run it under cold water to cool.

3 Mix together the remaining oil and the lemon juice. Toss the broccoli, pomegranate seeds and pumpkin seeds through the couscous with the lemon dressing. At the last moment, roughly chop the watercress and toss through the couscous.

4 Serve with the salmon, lemon wedges for squeezing over and extra olive oil for drizzling.

• Per serving 522 kcalories, protein 39g, carbohydrate 34g, fat 27g, saturated fat 5g, fibre 6g, sugar 8g, salt 0.25g

If you're watching your waistline, with a little clever cooking these creamy chicken pies needn't be out of bounds – they are less than 350 calories each.

Chicken and leek pot pies

500g/1lb 2oz parsnips, peeled and cut into small chunks
300g/10oz floury potatoes, peeled and cut into small chunks
500g/1lb 2oz boneless skinless chicken breasts
2 tsp cornflour
1 tbsp olive oil
1 leek, sliced
zest of 1 lemon
2 tbsp chopped fresh parsley
2 tbsp low-fat crème fraîche
1 tbsp wholegrain mustard

Takes 30 minutes • Serves 4

1 Boil the parsnips and potatoes together for 15 minutes until tender. Drain, reserving the water, then mash with a little seasoning.
2 Cut the chicken into small chunks, then toss them in the cornflour. Heat the oil in a large pan, add the leeks, then fry them for 3 minutes until starting to soften. Add the chicken and 200ml/7fl oz water from the cooking, then bring to the boil, stirring. Reduce the heat, then gently simmer for 10 minutes, until the chicken is just tender.
3 Remove from the heat, then stir in the lemon zest, parsley, crème fraîche and mustard. Heat the grill to medium.
4 Divide the chicken filling among four 300ml/½ pint pie dishes. Spoon over the mash and spread roughly with a fork to seal in the filling. Grill for 5 minutes or until golden.

• Per serving 331 kcalories, protein 36g, carbohydrate 34g, fat 7g, saturated fat 1g, fibre 9g, sugar 10g, salt 0.25g

If you like peanut satay chicken, you'll love this quick
and tasty supper.

Nutty chicken with noodle salad

140g/5oz unsalted roasted peanuts
4 skinless chicken breasts, halved
lengthways
1 egg, lightly beaten with a fork
85g/3oz dried soba or buckwheat
noodles
1 cucumber, halved and sliced
1 small bunch of fresh mint, leaves
picked and larger ones roughly
chopped
zest and juice of 2 limes
1–2 tsp sugar
1 red chilli, seeded and finely sliced
(optional)

Takes 30 minutes • Serves 4

1 Preheat the oven to 200°C/180°C fan/
gas 6 and cover a baking sheet with baking
parchment.
2 Finely chop the peanuts in a food
processor or by hand – you want large
crumbs, not dust – then tip on to a plate.
Dip the chicken pieces in the egg, then coat
in the peanuts and put on the baking sheet.
Bake for 15–18 minutes until golden and
cooked through.
3 Meanwhile, cook the noodles according to
the packet instructions, drain, rinse under cold
water until cool, then drain again. When the
chicken is cooked, use kitchen tongs or two
forks to mix the noodles with the cucumber
slices, mint leaves, lime juice and zest, sugar,
chilli (if using) and some seasoning. Serve
immediately, topped with the crunchy chicken.

• Per serving 483 kcalories, protein 49g, carbohydrate
24g, fat 22g, saturated fat 5g, fibre 3g, sugar 5g,
salt 0.70g

Orange and fennel give plenty of flavour and texture to winter salads. Set this lusciously low-fat salmon on a platter on the table and let everyone just dig in.

Salmon, fennel and orange salad

4 small or 2 large salmon fillets
100g bag fresh watercress
410g can chickpeas, drained and rinsed
1 fennel bulb, thinly sliced
½ red onion, thinly sliced
2 oranges
100g/3½oz natural yogurt
2 tbsp chopped dill, plus a few fronds to garnish

Takes 15 minutes • Serves 4

1 Put the salmon in a microwave-proof dish, cover with cling film, then cook on High for 3½–4 minutes until the salmon is just cooked. Peel the skin away and flake into large chunks.
2 Toss together the watercress, chickpeas, fennel and onion, then arrange on a large platter. Zest one of the oranges, cut away the white pith and flesh from each orange, then segment them both and add to the salad. Squeeze the juice from the leftover middle section of the oranges into a bowl and mix two tablespoons of it with the yogurt, dill, zest and seasoning.
3 Scatter the salmon chunks over the salad, then serve with the creamy orange dressing drizzled on top.

• Per serving 369 kcalories, protein 34g, carbohydrate 24g, fat 16g, saturated fat 3g, fibre 6g, sugar 14g, salt 0.59g

A brilliantly tasty, cheap supper that's on the table in under half an hour.

Spaghetti with leeks, peas and pesto

175g/6oz spaghetti
140g/5oz frozen peas
1 tbsp olive oil
2 large trimmed leeks (about 250g/9oz), thinly sliced
1 tbsp basil pesto
freshly grated Parmesan, to serve (optional)

Takes 25 minutes • Serves 2 (easily doubled)

1 Cook the spaghetti according to the packet instructions, adding the peas for the final 2 minutes.

2 Meanwhile, heat the oil in a frying pan, add the leeks, then gently cook for about 5 minutes until softened. Stir in the pesto and three tablespoons of the pasta cooking water, then simmer for a few minutes.

3 Drain the pasta and peas, then add to the frying pan, tossing everything together. Divide between two warm bowls and sprinkle with a little grated Parmesan, if using.

• Per serving 447 kcalories, protein 18g, carbohydrate 75g, fat 10g, saturated fat 2g, fibre 9g, sugar 8g, salt 0.11g

Once you've tried this Thai-stuffed chicken, you'll make it again and again. It goes perfectly with plain rice.

Thai roast chicken with mango and apple salad

3 shallots, halved
2 small red chillies, seeded, 1 roughly chopped, 1 finely chopped
zest and juice of 1 lime
thumb-length knob of fresh root ginger, roughly chopped
2 tsp sunflower oil
2 chicken breasts, skin on

■■ ■■ ■■■ ■ ■■ ■■■

1 red-skinned apple, cut into matchsticks
½ mango, peeled and cut into matchsticks
½ small bunch of mint, leaves picked
3 spring onions, sliced
1 small bunch of fresh coriander, leaves picked
½ tsp fish sauce, plus a splash
¼ tsp caster sugar

Takes 30 minutes • Serves 2 (easily doubled)

1 Whiz the shallots, roughly chopped chilli, lime zest and ginger in a food processor to a chunky paste. Fry the paste in a teaspoon of oil for a couple of minutes until fragrant. Season.
2 Preheat the oven to 200°C/180°C fan/gas 6. Release the skin from the chicken breasts, stuff the shallot mix underneath, season, then roast in a roasting tin for 15–20 minutes.
3 Meanwhile, make the salad. Toss the apple, mango, mint leaves, spring onions and half the coriander in a bowl. Mix together the fish sauce, caster sugar and half the lime juice; set aside.
4 Rest the chicken on a plate. Scoop out the fat from the pan, then gently heat the juices, the remaining lime juice and a splash more fish sauce. Chop the remaining coriander and stir into the sauce with the finely chopped chilli. Toss the salad with the dressing, then serve with the chicken and sauce.

• Per serving 275 kcalories, protein 33g, carbohydrate 22g, fat 7g, saturated fat 2g, fibre 4g, sugar 20g, salt 0.80g

Pep up weeknight pork with a simple, spicy marinade.

Pork and mushroom kebabs with quick fried rice

1 tsp Thai curry paste
1 tsp light muscovado sugar
2 × 125g pots low-fat natural yogurt
400g/14oz lean pork fillet, cut into cubes
300g/10oz chestnut mushrooms
1 tbsp sunflower oil
2 spring onions, finely chopped
2cm knob fresh root ginger, finely chopped
200g/8oz basmati rice, cooked and cooled
100g/4oz sugar snap peas, shredded
175g/6oz frozen sweetcorn (or from a can)
good pinch of paprika
lemon or lime wedges, to serve

Takes 30 minutes • Serves 4

1 Blend the Thai paste, sugar and half the yogurt in a large bowl. Add the pork and mushrooms. Mix well, then thread on to eight pre-soaked wooden skewers.

2 Cook the kebabs under a hot grill for 6–8 minutes, turning once. Meanwhile, heat the oil in a non-stick pan or wok, add the spring onions and ginger, then briefly fry. Add the rice, peas, sweetcorn and paprika, then stir-fry for 2–3 minutes. Serve with the kebabs, the rest of the yogurt and lemon or lime wedges.

• Per serving 421 kcalories, protein 33g, carbohydrate 56g, fat 9g, saturated fat 2g, fibre 2g, sugar 8g, salt 0.37g

Simple grilled chicken in a tangy tamarind glaze goes brilliantly with a pile of creamy, spicy mashed potatoes.

Tamarind chicken with golden mash

1kg/2lb 4oz potatoes, peeled and cubed
2 tsp ground turmeric
500g/1lb 2oz broccoli
4 tsp tamarind paste
2 tbsp mango chutney
4 skinless chicken breasts
100g/3½oz natural yogurt
1 tbsp korma paste
5 spring onions, trimmed and thinly sliced

Takes 30 minutes • Serves 4

1 Heat the grill. Put the potatoes in a pan of cold water, stir in the turmeric, then bring to the boil. Simmer for 12–15 minutes until tender. Steam the broccoli in a metal colander or sieve over the potato pan for 4–5 minutes until tender.

2 Mix together the tamarind paste and mango chutney. Make a few slashes in each chicken breast and place on a baking sheet. Brush with the tamarind mixture, then grill for 5 minutes on each side or until cooked through and sticky.

3 Drain the potatoes. Mash with the yogurt, korma paste and seasoning, then keep warm. To serve, stir most of the spring onions into the mash, then spoon on to plates. Scatter with the remaining spring onions and serve alongside the chicken and broccoli.

• Per serving 394 kcalories, protein 41g, carbohydrate 53g, fat 3g, saturated fat 1g, fibre 3g, sugar 10g, salt 0.70g

Roasting carrots brings out their natural sweetness. Together with tangy, salty feta they make a fabulous salad that's ideal for lunchboxes too.

Caraway-roasted carrot and feta salad

300g/10oz carrots, peeled and halved or quartered lengthways
1 tsp caraway seeds
2 tbsp olive oil
1 orange
2 tsp red wine vinegar
1 tbsp mixed seeds, such as pumpkin, sunflower and linseed
2 large handfuls of baby leaf spinach
50g/2oz feta

Takes 30 minutes • Serves 2 (easily doubled)

1 Preheat the oven to 200°C/180°C fan/gas 6.

2 Cook the carrots in a pan of boiling water for 4 minutes. Drain, tip on to a baking sheet, then toss with the caraway seeds, a teaspoon of oil, the zest from the orange and seasoning. Roast for 20 minutes until golden and tender.

3 Meanwhile, cut away the pith from the orange. Hold the orange over a bowl, then cut free each segment, catching the juice and segments in the bowl. Squeeze out any remaining juice from the leftover bits of orange, then add the remaining oil, the vinegar, seeds and seasoning. Stir, then combine with the roasted carrots and spinach. Divide between two plates and crumble over the feta.

• Per serving 221 kcalories, protein 9g, carbohydrate 22g, fat 12g, saturated fat 4g, fibre 6g, sugar 19g, salt 1.2g

Give the family something hearty but healthy with this warming cobbler.

Ham and leek cobbler

2½ tbsp olive oil
450g/1lb leeks, trimmed and thickly sliced
460ml/16fl oz vegetable stock
100g/4oz self-raising flour, plus a little extra for rolling the dough
75g/2½oz fat-free natural yogurt
1 tsp fresh thyme leaves, plus extra to garnish
140g/5oz frozen peas
85g/3oz thick-cut ham, shredded
1 small or ½ large apple, grated

Takes 30 minutes • Serves 4

1 Preheat the oven to 200°C/180°C fan/gas 6. Heat the half tablespoon of oil in a large pan, then fry the leeks, stirring, for 5 minutes until starting to soften. Add the stock, then simmer for 5 minutes.

2 Meanwhile, tip the flour into a bowl, make a well in the centre, then add the yogurt, remaining oil, thyme leaves and a little salt. Using a cutlery knife, mix to bring together to a soft dough. Divide into four and shape into rounds on a floured surface.

3 Stir the peas, ham and grated apple into the leeks, then divide among four individual pie dishes (or spoon into one large dish). Top each with a round of dough (or dot around the large dish), scatter with more thyme, then bake for 15 minutes or until golden and crisp.

• Per serving 255 kcalories, protein 12g, carbohydrate 32g, fat 9g, saturated fat 2g, fibre 6g, sugar 8g, salt 1.02g

This easy-to-make dish is low in fat and spiked with a little chilli – a great all-rounder that will satisfy your hunger and your tastebuds.

Grilled chilli and coriander salmon with ginger rice

2 skinless salmon fillets, (each about 140g/5oz)
1 red chilli, seeded and finely chopped
a small bunch of fresh coriander, chopped
1 lime, halved, to serve

FOR THE RICE
2 tbsp olive oil
1 onion, chopped
a small knob of fresh root ginger, finely chopped
1 garlic clove, thinly sliced
100g/4oz basmati rice

Takes 20 minutes • Serves 2

1 First, make the rice. Boil the kettle. Heat a tablespoon of oil in a pan and fry the onion for a few minutes until lightly browned. Stir in the ginger and garlic, fry for 1 minute, then stir in the rice. Add 300ml/10fl oz boiling water and a little salt, then bring to the boil. Cover and cook for 10–12 minutes until the rice is tender. Heat the grill to medium.
2 Brush a baking sheet lightly with a little oil. Put the salmon on top and grill for 4–5 minutes, then scatter with the chilli, coriander, remaining olive oil and seasoning. Grill again for just 4–5 minutes until the salmon is cooked through. Serve with the rice and lime halves for squeezing over.

• Per serving 546 kcalories, protein 33g, carbohydrate 46g, fat 27g, saturated fat 5g, fibre 1g, sugar 4g, salt 0.17g

Using raspberries from the freezer makes this pudding a cinch to prepare, any time of year.

Effortless raspberry iced mousse

2 × 250g tubs Quark
50g/2oz icing sugar
a squeeze or two of fresh lemon juice
250g pack frozen raspberries,

Takes 5 minutes • Serves 4

1 Tip the Quark and sugar into a large bowl, squeeze in a few drops of lemon juice and beat with a wooden spoon until smooth and creamy (you can do this an hour or two ahead, if you have time).
2 Gently stir in the raspberries until they begin to break up and the mixture is streaked pink. Taste and add a little more lemon juice, if liked. Spoon into four glasses and serve.

• Per serving 158 kcalories, protein 19g, carbohydrate 21g, fat none, saturated fat none, fibre 2g, added sugar 13g, salt 0.17g

Just a few spoonfuls of this rich and creamy dessert are all you need to end a romantic meal with a flourish.

Tia Maria and chocolate creams

50g/2oz dark chocolate (70% cocoa solids), broken into squares
150ml/¼ pint double cream
2 tbsp Tia Maria (or use Kahlua, Cointreau or Grand Marnier)
cocoa powder, for dusting
cantuccini or amaretti biscuits, to serve

Takes 30 minutes • Serves 2 (easily doubled)

1 Put the chocolate into a bowl. Reserve two tablespoons of cream, then mix the rest with the liqueur of your choice, tip into a pan and bring just to the boil. Remove from the heat and pour over the chocolate, stirring until the chocolate melts. Divide between two small glasses and allow to cool slightly.
2 Whip the reserved cream until slightly thickened, then spoon over the cooled chocolate mix. Chill for at least 20 minutes until set. While you're waiting, cut a heart shape from a piece of thick card.
3 When ready to serve, set the heart template over the top of the glass and sift over a dusting of cocoa powder. Lift off carefully and do the same with the other glass. Serve with cantuccini or amaretti biscuits, if you like.

• Per serving 566 kcalories, protein 3g, carbohydrate 17g, fat 51g, saturated fat 28g, fibre 2g, sugar 12g, salt 0.05g

A family favourite for winter that's ready in no time.

Caramel apple crumble

8 eating apples, peeled, cored
and cubed
6 tbsp caramel cream (from a can or
squeezy tube)
50g/2oz plain flour
50g/2oz porridge oats
50g/2oz cold butter, diced

Takes 30 minutes • Serves 4

1 Preheat the oven to 220°C/200°C fan/
gas 7. Put the apples into a pan with a
splash of water, cover, then cook over a
high heat for 4–5 minutes, stirring now and
then until just soft. Stir in three tablespoons
of the caramel, then tip the mixture into small
ovenproof dishes. Reserve a tablespoon of
caramel, then dot the rest in small spoonfuls
over the apples.
2 Mix together the flour and oats, then rub
in the butter with your fingers until you have
a crumbly mixture. Stir in the remaining
caramel, then scatter this over the apples.
Bake for 15 minutes until golden and crisp
on top.

• Per serving 340 kcalories, protein 5g, carbohydrate
54g, fat 13g, saturated fat 8g, fibre 5g, sugar 36g,
salt 0.27g

These cute little puds are irresistible with a scoop of ice cream. If your coffee cups are made of delicate china, use deep ramekins instead.

Warm honey cup puddings

2 tbsp butter, melted, plus extra for greasing the cups
2 tsp clear honey, plus extra for drizzling
50g/2oz self-raising flour
25g/1oz ground almonds
50g/2oz light muscovado sugar
¼ tsp bicarbonate of soda
1 large egg
85g/3oz Greek yogurt
1 tbsp pistachio nuts, roughly chopped, to sprinkle
ice cream, to serve

Takes 25 minutes • Serves 2

1 Butter two large coffee cups or individual ramekins, then line the bottoms with a circle of non-stick baking paper. Add a teaspoon of honey to the bottom of each.
2 Preheat the oven to 180°C/160°C fan/gas 4. Mix the dry ingredients in a large bowl, squashing any lumps of sugar. Beat the egg, melted butter and yogurt together, then stir into the dry mix until smooth. Spoon the mix into the cups, sit them on a baking sheet, then bake for 20 minutes until risen and golden. Test if they're ready by inserting a skewer – it should come out clean.
3 Loosen the edge of each pud with a round-bladed knife, then up-turn them on to serving plates. Remove the lining disc, drizzle over a little more honey, then serve with ice cream and a sprinkling of pistachios.

• Per serving 545 kcalories, protein 13g, carbohydrate 55g, fat 32g, saturated fat 13g, fibre 2g, sugar 35g, salt 1.14g

Treat yourself to this fruity compote – it's so good you'll want it with everything.

Warm berry compote

a knob of butter
2 tbsp caster sugar
1 tsp vanilla extract
200g punnet fresh raspberries
200g punnet fresh blueberries
vanilla ice cream, to serve

Takes 10 minutes • Serves 4

1 Melt the butter over a low heat. Stir in the sugar and vanilla extract, then cook until the sugar melts. Toss in the raspberries and blueberries; give them a good shake, then cook for 2–3 minutes until the fruit starts to soften. Serve warm with vanilla ice cream.

• Per serving 232 kcalories, protein 1g, carbohydrate 21g, fat 11g, saturated fat 7g, fibre 1g, sugar 21g, salt 0.18g

As these puddings sit in the fridge the sugar dissolves into a delicious caramel – a sure-fire hit with kids and grownups.

Banana yogurt pots

450g pot thick natural yogurt
3–4 bananas, cut into chunks
4 tbsp soft dark brown sugar
25g/1oz pecan nuts, chopped

Takes 25 minutes • Serves 4

1 Dollop about one tablespoon of yogurt into the bottom of four small glasses. Add a layer of banana, then some more yogurt. Repeat the layers until the glasses are full
2 Scatter over the sugar and nuts, then leave in the fridge for 20 minutes until the sugar has dissolved.

• Per serving 230 kcalories, protein 7g, carbohydrate 40g, fat 6g, saturated fat 1g, fibre 1g, added sugar 39g, salt 0.23g

Ready-rolled pastry cuts the prep time needed for these light and spicy little tarts.

Rhubarb puffs with oaty streusel topping

5 rhubarb sticks, cut into 3cm pieces
1 tsp ground cinnamon
3 tbsp plain flour, plus extra for dusting
5 tbsp soft brown sugar
½ × 500g block puff pastry, defrosted if frozen
3 tbsp unsalted butter
50g/2oz rolled oats

Takes 30 minutes, plus defrosting
Serves 4

1 Preheat the oven to 200°C/180°C fan/gas 6. In a bowl, toss the rhubarb with the cinnamon, one tablespoon of flour and two tablespoons of sugar.

2 Line a baking sheet with a piece of baking parchment. Roll out the pastry on a floured surface to about 20cm x 30cm, then cut into quarters and place on the lined sheet.

3 Rub together the remaining flour, sugar, butter and oats to make a rough crumble mixture. Divide the rhubarb among the pastry quarters, leaving a 1cm rim. Sprinkle the crumble mixture over, then fold and pinch each corner to keep the filling in. Bake for 20 minutes, and serve warm.

• Per serving 465 kcalories, protein 6g, carbohydrate 53g, fat 27g, saturated fat 13g, fibre 3g, sugar 21g, salt 0.57g

Ready in no time at all, this sophisticated dessert is a real summertime treat.

Sweet wine and sorbet

500ml tub good-quality peach or
mango sorbet
8 tbsp sweet dessert wine
8 thin crisp biscuits, to serve

Takes 2 minutes, plus 10 minutes
softening • Serves 4 (easily halved)

1 Remove the sorbet from the freezer 10 minutes before you want to serve it, to let it soften.

2 Put a couple of scoops of the sorbet into four serving bowls. Pour a few tablespoons of wine over each bowlful, then serve straight away with crisp biscuits to dunk.

22g, fat 0.2g, saturated fat none, fibre none, sugar 21g, salt 0.03g

Finish an Italian meal in style with these quick
tiramisu-flavoured puds.

Chocolate creams with espresso and Vin Santo

250g tub mascarpone
4 tsp icing sugar
200ml/8fl oz fresh vanilla custard
(from a 500ml pot)
25g/1oz dark chocolate, grated
zest of 1 orange

TO SERVE
6 cups strong espresso or six cups
strong coffee
37.5cl bottle Vin Santo (enough for
6 glasses)
250g pack cantuccini or biscotti
biscuits

Takes 10 minutes • Serves 6

1 Tip the mascarpone into a bowl and beat
with a wooden spoon to soften. Add the icing
sugar and custard, stirring until smooth. Fold
in the chocolate and orange zest. Spoon into
six small glasses, cover and chill until needed.
2 When ready to serve, prepare the coffee.
Serve the coffee alongside the chocolate
creams, with a glass of Vin Santo and
biscuits for dipping.

• Per serving 263 kcalories, protein 3g, carbohydrate
13g, fat 23g, saturated fat 14g, fibre none, sugar 10g,
salt 0.15g

It's easy to transform storecupboard dried fruits into an indulgent
compote with just a little fresh orange juice and some warming spices.

10-minute winter fruit compote

500g pack dried mixed fruit
200ml/7fl oz fresh orange juice
½ cinnamon stick
6 whole cloves
6 black peppercorns
0% Greek yogurt or low-fat fromage
frais, to serve

Takes 10 minutes • Serves 4

1 Tip the dried fruit, orange juice and
whole spices into a microwave-proof bowl.
Microwave on High for 4–5 minutes, stirring
halfway through until the juices become sticky
and the fruits are plump.
2 Leave the compote to stand for a minute
and serve in bowls with spoonfuls of yogurt
or fromage frais.

• Per serving 352 kcalories, protein 3g, carbohydrate
89g, fat 1g, saturated fat none, fibre 3g, added sugar
none, salt 0.15g

A classic syllabub, made special here with the addition of rosé wine and zesty lime, really complements a bowl of sweetened fresh strawberries.

Rosé syllabub and sugared strawberries

700g/1lb 9oz fresh strawberries, halved if large
3 tbsp golden caster sugar
½ bottle/375ml rosé wine

FOR THE ROSÉ SYLLABUB
125ml/4fl oz rosé wine, well chilled
50g/2oz golden caster sugar
finely grated zest and juice of 1 lime, plus extra zest to decorate
284ml pot double cream

Takes 20 minutes • Serves 6

1 Put the strawberries in a bowl and sprinkle over the sugar; let them sit for 10 minutes, stir, then pour over the wine and leave for 10 minutes more.

2 Meanwhile, make the syllabub. Put the wine, sugar, lime zest and juice in a jug Half-whip the cream, then gradually pour in the chilled-wine mix, continuing to beat until it all comes together in a thick, creamy mixture.

3 Serve the strawberries and their boozy juice in bowls topped with a spoonful of syllabub, and scatter over a little lime zest.

• Per serving 387 kcalories, protein 2g, carbohydrate 27g, fat 26g, saturated fat 14g, fibre 1g, sugar 27g, salt 0.05g

Index

Picture and recipe credits

BBC *Good Food* magazine would like to thank the following people for providing photos. While every effort has been made to trace and acknowledge all photographers, we should like to apologize should there be any errors or omissions.

Marie-Louise Avery p157; Peter Cassidy p95; Dean Grennan p15; William Lingwood p111, p181; Gareth Morgans p23, p43, p53, p00, p01, p00, p100, p115, p131, p135, p139, p165, p167, p171, p199; David Munns p47, p117, p119, p141, p179, p191, p203; Myles New p11, p17, p19, p21, p25, p35, p41, p49, p59, p61, p63, p65, p67, p71, p73, p97, p99, p101, p109, p137, p145, p155, p169, p175, p189, p197; Lis Parsons p13, p27, p29, p33, p37, p45, p69, p77, p81, p83, p85, p87, p105, p113, p121, p123, p125, p147, p149, p153, p161, p163, p173, p177, p193, p195, p205; Craig Robertson p207; Brett Stevens p39, p51, p57; Roger Stowell p127, p159; Yuki Sugiura p31; Dawie Verwey p79, p107, p143, p151, p183, p185, p187; Simon Walton p201; Philip Webb p75, p129, p133, p209, p211; Kate Whitaker p55

All the recipes in this book were created by the editorial team at *Good Food* and by regular contributors to the magazine